YORK NOTES

Twelfth Night

William Shakespeare

Notes by David Pinnington

 Longman   ⊛ York Press

YORK PRESS
322 Old Brompton Road, London SW5 9JH

ADDISON WESLEY LONGMAN LIMITED
Edinburgh Gate, Harlow,
Essex CM20 2JE, United Kingdom
Associated companies, branches and representatives throughout the world

First published 1997

ISBN 0–582–31530–1

Illustrated by Tony Chance
Designed by Vicki Pacey, Trojan Horse
Phototypeset by Gem Graphics, Trenance, Mawgan Porth, Cornwall
Produced by Longman Asia Limited, Hong Kong

CONTENTS

PREFACE

York Notes are designed to give you a broader perspective on works of literature studied at GCSE and equivalent levels. We have carried out extensive research into the needs of the modern literature student prior to publishing this new edition. Our research showed that no existing series fully met students' requirements. Rather than present a single authoritative approach, we have provided alternative viewpoints, empowering students to reach their own interpretations of the text. York Notes provide a close examination of the work and include biographical and historical background, summaries, glossaries, analyses of characters, themes, structure and language, cultural connections and literary terms.

If you look at the Contents page you will see the structure for the series. However, there's no need to read from the beginning to the end as you would with a novel, play, poem or short story. Use the Notes in the way that suits you. Our aim is to help you with your understanding of the work, not to dictate how you should learn.

York Notes are written by English teachers and examiners, with an expert knowledge of the subject. They show you how to succeed in coursework and examination assignments, guiding you through the text and offering practical advice. Questions and comments will extend, test and reinforce your knowledge. Attractive colour design and illustrations improve clarity and understanding, making these Notes easy to use and handy for quick reference.

York Notes are ideal for:

- Essay writing
- Exam preparation
- Class discussion

The author of these Notes is David Pinnington. David read English at the universities of York and Exeter, where he took an MA in Modern Fiction. He teaches in Devon and is a Senior GCSE Examiner for English and English Literature.

The text used in these Notes is the Arden Shakespeare Series, Routledge 1975.

Health Warning: **This study guide will enhance your understanding, but should not replace the reading of the original text and/or study in class.**

PART ONE

INTRODUCTION

HOW TO STUDY A PLAY

You have bought this book because you wanted to study a play on your own. This may supplement classwork.

- Drama is a special 'kind' of writing (the technical term is 'genre') because it needs a performance in the theatre to arrive at a full interpretation of its meaning. When reading a play you have to imagine how it should be performed; the words alone will not be sufficient. Think of gestures and movements.

- Drama is always about conflict of some sort (it may be below the surface). Identify the conflicts in the play and you will be close to identifying the large ideas or themes which bind all the parts together.

- Make careful notes on themes, characters, plot and any sub-plots of the play.

- Playwrights find non-realistic ways of allowing an audience to see into the minds and motives of their characters. The 'soliloquy', in which a character speaks directly to the audience, is one such device. Does the play you are studying have any such passages?

- Which characters do you like or dislike in the play? Why? Do your sympathies change as you see more of these characters?

- Think of the playwright writing the play. Why were these particular arrangements of events, these particular sets of characters and these particular speeches chosen?

Studying on your own requires self-discipline and a carefully thought-out work plan in order to be effective. Good luck.

Family life	William Shakespeare was born at Stratford-upon-Avon in 1564. There is a record of his christening, 26 April, so we can assume he was born shortly before that date. His father, John Shakespeare, was a glove-maker and trader who later became high bailiff of Stratford; his mother, Mary Arden, was the daughter of a landowner. It is probable that William would have attended the local grammar school where the curriculum included Latin rhetoric, logic and literature.

In 1582 Shakespeare married Anne Hathaway, a woman eight years older than himself, and their first child, Susanna, was christened in May 1583. Two other children were born to Anne and William in 1585, the twins Hamnet and Judith. Both Shakespeare's daughters lived to marry and produce children, but Hamnet only lived till he was eleven – his burial took place in Stratford on 11 August 1596.

Writing	Sometime after 1585 Shakespeare left Stratford and went to London where he became an actor and a dramatist. He worked first with a group of actors called Lord Pembroke's Men and later with a company called the Lord Chamberlain's Men (later the King's Men). His earliest plays, *Henry IV Parts 1–3*, *Richard III*, *Titus Andronicus* and the comedies *The Comedy of Errors*, *The Taming of the Shrew* and *The Two Gentlemen of Verona* were performed around 1590–4. Shakespeare was very successful in the theatre from the start and his genius inspired the resentment of one man, Robert Greene, a mediocre university-educated dramatist who described him to his friends as 'an upstart Crow, beautified with our feathers'.

In the 1590s Shakespeare wrote six more comedies, culminating in *Twelfth Night* in 1601. During this time he also wrote history plays, tragedies and the narrative poems, *Venus and Adonis* and *The Rape of Lucrece*, in addition to the Sonnets which were published in 1609. In the early years of the new century he turned his attentions almost exclusively to tragedy and wrote some of the most powerful works in this genre (see Literary Terms) that have ever existed: *Hamlet* (1604–5), *Othello* (1604–5), *Macbeth* (1605–6), *King Lear* (1606–7) and *Antony and Cleopatra* (1606–7).

Although Shakespeare lived and worked for most of his life in London, he obviously did not forget Stratford. In 1596 he acquired the right to a coat of arms there, something his father had tried and failed to do, and in 1597 he bought a large house in the town called New Place. Later, in 1602, he acquired other property, and in about 1610 he returned to live in Stratford permanently.

Play-writing occupied Shakespeare until the final years of his life and between 1608–12 he produced the so-called 'last plays', *Pericles*, *Cymbeline*, *The Winter's Tale* and *The Tempest*. These plays suggest a mellowing in outlook and a concern for the relationships of parents and children, as if they were written by a man who was taking stock of his life and thinking of the future generation who would replace him.

Shakespeare wrote a will in January 1616, leaving bequests to Stratford acquaintances and to his actor-friends, Burbage, Heminges and Condell. The latter pair edited the first complete edition of Shakespeare's works, the First Folio of 1623. He died on 23 April 1616.

CONTEXT & SETTING

The feast of 'Twelfth Night'

'Twelfth Night' was the name given to the last day of the Elizabethan Christmas celebrations, a feast day which was celebrated enthusiastically across the land. It ended a two-week series of festivities and in the Christian calendar is known as the Feast of Epiphany, a commemoration of the coming of the Magi to the stable in Bethlehem with their gifts of gold, frankincense and myrrh.

Shakespeare's title to his play, however, has nothing to do with its story and merely refers to when it was performed, probably 6 January 1602. It is likely that the alternative title, *What You Will*, also refers to the festive associations, a signal to the audience that the play is an entertainment for a special occasion.

Dramatic background	It is very likely that Shakespeare wrote *Twelfth Night* in 1601 – there are references in the play to events which had happened in or just before that year. When Fabian says that Sir Andrew has 'sailed into the north of my lady's (Olivia's) opinion, where you will hang like an icicle on a Dutchman's beard' (III.2.24–6) he is referring to the voyage to the Arctic of William Barent (1596–7); and the characterisation of Malvolio's smiling face by Maria, 'into more lines than is in the new map with the augmentation of the Indies' (III.2.76–7) is a reference to a map of the East Indies published in 1599–1600 and notable for its many odd lines radiating out from the centre.

The plot of *Twelfth Night* comes from two probable sources: a short story called *The Historie of Apolonius and Silla* and the Italian play, *Gl'Ingannati* (The Deceived Ones), a comedy of mistaken identity with only incidental love interest. Whatever the source of the play, it is the conventions which defined Elizabethan Romantic comedy that need to be borne in mind while studying *Twelfth Night*. A typical play might include the stock characters (see Literary Terms) of: a cunning servant who motivates much of the action; a pedant or hypocrite; a pair of young lovers; and twins. Confusions of identity were a common feature as was disguise, and transvestite disguise in particular. Because these elements were so common, Shakespeare's audience must have entered the theatre with their expectations clearly focused.

Malvolio and Puritanism

Twelfth Night was sometimes given the title *Malvolio* when it was subsequently performed in Shakespeare's day, such was the impression which this extraordinary character had on audiences. This impression, of course, is the result of the way Shakespeare has turned a character 'type' into a richly individualised portrait. Perhaps Malvolio is a caricature of the unpopular Sir William Knollys, Controller of Her Majesty's Household, in which case his treatment in the play would have special comic significance for the first Court audience; for the wider Elizabethan audience, it was the depiction of Malvolio as a Puritan that was relevant. The Puritans were a religious group who had condemned theatres and other entertainments because they thought they had a corrupting influence. They thought plays contained too much sex and violence, and were unchristian and the cause of sin. They dressed plainly, disliked drinking, and had a strict code of personal behaviour. Many of the Puritans in Shakespeare's time were connected to the merchant classes and were considered to be self-serving hypocrites. Malvolio thus embodies all the attributes which the pleasure-seeking Elizabethan audience was predisposed to hate. There is no explicit sympathy for him in the play whatsoever. The joke against him is curtailed by Sir Toby out of self-interest, and Olivia's comment at the end that he has been 'most notoriously abused' is a half-serious echo of Malvolio's own earlier phrase. However, Malvolio's final threat of revenge reverberates beyond the immediate context of the play: the Puritans succeeded in closing down the theatres in 1642.

Think of some modern-day Malvolio who would like to impose their moral standards on everybody else.

A distant setting is common to Elizabethan romantic comedy.

Only a few simple stage properties were ever used in the Elizabethan theatre. The setting of each scene was created by a combination of words and music. When the sea captain tells Viola that 'This is Illyria, lady.' (I.2.2) it would have been in front of an audience who were willing to let their imaginations be acted upon by language. The country of Illyria may have been an actual place (now a part of former Yugoslavia) but to the Elizabethan audience its name evoked an almost magical region, far away from the real world, where all the improbabilities of the story could be accepted.

The setting of *Twelfth Night* is relevant to its themes of love, disguise and deception. Two houses and rather formal gardens have to be imagined within which the characters seem separated from one another by the preoccupations of their respective plots and the limitations of their own understanding. Beyond this the hostile and unfathomable sea roars, the sea which for Orsino is like the 'spirit of love' and which has brought Viola and Sebastian to the shores of Illyria.

PART TWO

SUMMARIES

GENERAL SUMMARY

Act I

In Illyria Duke Orsino reflects on his love for Olivia. He awaits the return of a messenger (Valentine) to her. Valentine tells him that Olivia has vowed to mourn her brother's death for seven years. Orsino regards it as proof of her love for him!

Viola and Sebastian are shipwrecked on the shores of Illyria.

In the meantime, in a shipwreck off the coast of Illyria, two identical twins have been separated. The female twin, Viola, is told that her brother, Sebastian, is probably dead. Viola decides, for safety's sake, to disguise herself as a eunuch and go and serve the Duke Orsino in his court.

Sir Toby Belch, the uncle of Olivia, lives in her house and is outraged by her decision to go into mourning, especially since he wants his friend, Sir Andrew Aguecheek, to seek her hand in marriage. Viola (disguised as the man Cesario) finds employment with Duke Orsino as love-messenger between him and Olivia. However, Viola finds herself secretly falling in love with Orsino.

Cesario (Viola) arrives with his mission to woo Olivia for Orsino and Olivia consents to see him. However, although she encourages Cesario to return, she forbids him to pursue the matter further. To make Cesario come back, Olivia sends Malvolio (her humourless and self-important steward) after him with a ring which she pretends he has left behind.

Act II

Viola's twin brother, Sebastian, has been rescued by Antonio but believes that his sister may have perished. He is in despair and decides to go to Orsino's court, and Antonio, an old enemy of Orsino, follows him.

After Malvolio has given the ring to 'Cesario', Viola realises that Olivia has fallen in love with 'him'.

A trick is played on Malvolio.

Sir Toby and Sir Andrew are drinking and singing when they are joined by Maria (a servant) and the clown, Feste. Malvolio interrupts them and tells them that Olivia wants them to quieten down. Resentful of Malvolio's arrogant attitude, Maria proposes a plan to make a fool of him. She will forge a love letter in Olivia's handwriting and leave it for Malvolio to find.

Meanwhile, Orsino finds he trusts and likes Cesario (Viola) greatly and tells the youth to convince Olivia of his love for her.

Malvolio imagines being married to his mistress and becoming Count Malvolio. He finds Maria's forged letter and becomes convinced that Olivia loves him. In the letter he finds a love-poem and some instructions on how he should behave and dress.

Act III

Olivia confesses to Cesario (Viola) that she has fallen in love with him but Cesario (Viola) rejects her.

Meanwhile, Sir Andrew Aguecheek has spied Olivia and Cesario together and become jealous. He is persuaded to challenge Cesario to a duel, though neither Sir Andrew nor Cesario (Viola) are fighting men.

On seeing the 'transformed' Malvolio, Olivia believes he has gone mad, and Sir Toby, Maria and Fabian (a servant) make plans to have him locked up in a 'dark room'.

Goaded and misled by Sir Toby and Fabian, Sir Andrew and Cesario (Viola) are brought together and forced to draw their swords. Antonio enters, and on seeing Cesario mistakenly believes it is Sebastian. He draws his sword and threatens to attack Sir Andrew and Sir Toby. Some of Orsino's officers arrive and arrest him. Antonio addresses Cesario as 'Sebastian' and the disguised Viola begins to hope that her twin brother is alive.

Act IV   Sebastian is mistaken for Cesario (Viola) and is attacked by Sir Andrew. Sebastian responds by beating the knight soundly. Olivia appears and also assumes that Sebastian is Cesario and talks to him lovingly after reprimanding her uncle, Sir Toby, for threatening to attack Sebastian. Olivia invites him in to her house and Sebastian follows her.

Meanwhile, Malvolio has been imprisoned and Maria and Feste play a new trick on him. Feste dresses up as a priest, and torments him. However, Sir Toby decides to bring the joke against Malvolio to an end and Feste agrees to help Malvolio explain to Olivia that he is not really mad.

Olivia summons a priest and marries Sebastian, still thinking that he is Cesario.

Act V   Orsino recognises Antonio who explains that he is not a pirate, and that he has rescued Sebastian, who (he believes) has disowned him just before he was arrested. He points accusingly at Cesario (Viola), thinking he is Sebastian.

Olivia appears and finally rejects Orsino, telling him that she has just married Cesario. Orsino threatens to kill Cesario, when Sir Andrew and Sir Toby appear claiming that Cesario (Viola) has assaulted them.

At last Sebastian enters and Viola (Cesario), recognising her lost brother, reveals her true identity. Olivia sends for Malvolio who learns the facts of his deception. He leaves, threatening revenge on all of them.

However, the play ends happily, for Sir Toby has married Maria, Olivia has married Sebastian, and the Duke Orsino promises to marry Viola.

ACT I

SCENE 1

How would you describe Orsino's character in this scene?

Consider how language contributes to the mood of the scene.

Orsino, Duke of Illyria, sits in his palace listening to music. He reflects on the many emotions that music inspires in people who are in love. The duke himself is in love with Olivia and his mood is sentimental and fanciful. He soon tires of the music and stops the musicians. He speaks of the 'spirit of love', its excessive needs and fickleness. Orsino's page, Curio, tries to distract him and asks if he would like to go hunting. The duke replies that he is already hunting the 'noblest' prey – Olivia. He is waiting for a reply to a message he has sent to her. When Valentine, the messenger, enters he has some disappointing news. Olivia's brother has died and she has vowed to mourn his death for seven years, during which time no one will see her face. Orsino is not put off by this. On the contrary, he thinks that if Olivia 'hath a heart of that fine frame' (line 33) to mourn a brother, then she would be even more sensitive and loyal to him as a lover.

COMMENT

The setting of the play is important. Shakespeare's comedies are set in distant places to intensify their romantic quality. Also, the softly sentimental music complements Orsino's very musical language, so underlining the theme of romance.

We learn about Orsino's attitude to love in this scene: he is as much in love with Olivia as he is with the idea of love itself. This revelling in emotion makes him appear a rather passive lover.

Notice the simile (see Literary Terms) of the sea to describe the 'spirit of love' which is never satisfied. At the end of the play Orsino will quickly change his affections from Olivia to Viola (V.1.265–6).

Two kinds of extreme emotion have been presented in this opening scene: Orsino's passion for Olivia and Olivia's vow to mourn for seven years. This encourages the audience to wonder if these feelings will survive.

GLOSSARY   **validity** value
                pitch height
                element air, sky
                cloistress nun

SCENE 2   On the seacoast of Illyria, Viola, a sea captain and some
                sailors have recently survived a shipwreck. The captain
                tells Viola that he saw her twin brother, Sebastian,
                tying himself to a mast just before the boat was split in
                two. The captain watched Sebastian being swept away
                by the waves and thinks that, although it is possible he
                survived, it is more likely that they are the only
                survivors. For giving her some small hope that her
                brother might be alive, Viola rewards the captain with
                gold and asks him if he is familiar with the country they
                have landed in. He is, and says he was born and
                brought up 'Not three hours' travel from this place'
                (line 23). Viola learns that Illyria is governed by the
                'noble' Duke Orsino whose name she remembers her
                late father mention. He was a bachelor in those days
                and according to the captain still is, at least until
                recently. The captain has only just visited Illyria and
                heard that Orsino was seeking the love of the 'fair'
                Olivia. Viola asks about Olivia and the captain tells
                her that she is a 'virtuous maid' (a virgin) whose father
                died a year ago leaving her under the protection of a
                brother, who has also died recently. Since then she has
                turned her back on the world. Viola wishes she could
Apart from   serve Olivia, perhaps because she herself is also
enabling Viola to brotherless. The captain tells her that would be
protect herself in a impossible because Olivia will see no one. Viola devises
strange land,   a plan. She will serve the duke instead. She promises to
what are the   pay the captain if he will help her disguise herself as a
dramatic   eunuch and then take her to Orsino. She can sing, and
advantages of a   she plays many musical instruments; in this way she will
disguised   make the duke employ her. The captain agrees to help
character?   her.

COMMENT

Why are there points of similarity between Olivia and Viola?

Notice the similarities and the differences between Viola and what we have learned about Olivia at this stage. They are both brotherless, both recently orphaned. Their names make an almost exact anagram. Yet Olivia can express her grief publicly and Viola cannot – she has to work out a way to survive.

Viola's disguise begins a complicated series of concealments and confusions which continues throughout the play.

There is a reference to music in relation to the duke and Viola, perhaps suggesting that she and Orsino might eventually fall in love.

GLOSSARY

Elysium heaven

unfoldeth to my hope reinforces my hope (for my brother's safety)

murmur rumour

delivered disclosed

hard to compass difficult to achieve

allow prove

wit skill, ingenuity

SCENE 3

The scene shifts to Olivia's house where her uncle, Sir Toby Belch, is complaining about the way his niece is mourning her brother's death. He thinks she is overreacting. Maria, Olivia's servant, tells him that Olivia disapproves of his late nights, his clothes and his drinking bouts. She has also complained of the 'foolish knight' that Sir Toby has brought home to woo her. Sir Andrew Aguecheek is a stupid waster, says Maria, but Sir Toby will have none of it. Not only is Sir Andrew rich, he replies, but he can play the viola-di-gamba and speak three or four languages. Maria retorts that Sir Andrew is a fool, a quarreller, a coward and a drunkard. And just as Sir Toby is making the extravagant claim that all their drinking amounts to is a few healths to Olivia, Sir Andrew appears.

Think about Sir Toby's relationship to Olivia, Maria and Sir Andrew from what is given in this scene.

Sir Toby introduces the knight to Maria, who proceeds to make him look every bit as stupid as she has claimed. After she has gone Sir Toby discovers that his friend is feeling very pessimistic about his chances with Olivia and is threatening to ride home the next day. She will see no one, he says, and even if she did, she certainly would not want to have anything to do with him. Besides, adds Sir Andrew, the Count Orsino is wooing her. Sir Toby manages to persuade Aguecheek to stay for another month by telling him that he has heard Olivia say she would never marry an older, more intelligent and more important person than herself. Sir Toby prompts Sir Andrew to admit that he is a good dancer. They will have a lot of fun if he stays and shows off his steps. The two knights agree to continue their 'revels'.

COMMENT

A new set of characters is introduced and the play moves from a romantic world down to a more earthly, fun-loving one of 'downstairs' characters. Sir Toby's explosive first line reveals his relationship to Olivia and the kind of character he is – a man devoted to pleasure.

Note the way Maria handles both Sir Toby and Sir Andrew. She is clever at verbal sparring and her frank appraisal of them suggests the influential role she will play in the comic sub-plot (see Literary Terms) which is to follow.

The relationship of Sir Toby to Sir Andrew is clearly given here. Sir Andrew is Sir Toby's dupe. The 'three thousand ducats a year' (line 22) is a significant factor in their relationship because Sir Andrew finances Sir Toby's pleasures and must be kept happy.

Olivia has now two suitors: Duke Orsino and the ridiculous Sir Andrew Aguecheek, and Malvolio will later make a third. The comic sub-plot reflects the main plot.

GLOSSARY   **he'll have but a year in all these ducats** he'll waste all that money in a year
viol-de-gamboys viola di gamba, an instrument like a cello, held between the legs
substractors detractors
Accost be polite
Excellent, it hangs ... spin it off (a double entendre) a housewife could use Sir Andrew's hair to spin with; a prostitute might take him between the legs and give him venereal disease, which was believed to make the hair fall out
kickshawes trifles

SCENE 4   Viola, disguised as the eunuch, Cesario, has become a great favourite with the Duke Orsino, even though he has known 'him' for only three days. Taking Cesario aside, Orsino commands him to carry love messages to Olivia. He urges the youth to be persistent, even to the point of discourtesy, until Olivia agrees to receive him. Cesario must describe to Olivia, Orsino's passion and his sorrow. The duke believes that because Cesario is so young and handsome – in voice and looks almost like a young girl himself – Olivia is more likely to respond favourably. Cesario will be rewarded well if he is successful. In a revealing aside Cesario (Viola) bemoans a situation in which she will be wooing for a man whom she herself would like to marry.

COMMENT   There is a distinct contrast between Orsino as a suitor for Olivia and Sir Andrew in the previous scene. The duke cannot help but look favourably against the absurd knight.

This is the first
time we see Viola
as 'Cesario'.

The extent of Orsino's confidence in Cesario is clear from the way he dismisses the other courtiers so that they can be alone together.

Orsino regards Cesario more as an intimate friend than a mere servant. This anticipates and makes possible their later relationship.

We need to be alert to the concept of dramatic irony (see Literary Terms): when the duke speaks admiringly of Cesario's feminine appearance and promises that he shall 'live as freely as thy lord' (line 39) he speaks more than he knows.

Viola's declaration that she herself loves the duke also prepares the audience for the ending. Yet one word, 'barful', indicates her awareness of the problems which this love has yet to encounter before its fulfillment.

GLOSSARY   **humour** changeable disposition
no less but all everything
address thy gait direct your steps
nuncio's messenger's
rubious ruby-red
semblative like
barful full of hindrances

SCENE 5   In Olivia's house Maria is telling Feste, the clown, that Olivia is annoyed by his absence. She wants to know where he has been and jokes that Olivia will hang him for playing truant. Feste does not care. 'Many a good hanging prevents a bad marriage' (line 19), he says. Maria advises him to have a good excuse prepared

Notice how Shakespeare builds up a picture of Olivia's character and situation in this scene.

because Olivia is about to appear. When Olivia enters, accompanied by her steward, Malvolio, she is very solemn and in no mood to listen to the prattling clown. She orders him away, but Feste embarks on some repartee that eventually amuses her and softens her towards him. Malvolio, however, finds the clown's joking impertinent and humourless. He wonders why Olivia finds such pleasure in someone so feeble in mind and body. Olivia responds by reproving Malvolio for his pride and intolerance. There is no offence in Feste's joking, she says, because he is an 'allowed fool', permitted to make harmless jests.

Maria announces that a handsome young gentleman has arrived who wishes to speak with Olivia, but he is being delayed at the gate by Sir Toby Belch. Olivia instructs Maria to fetch her uncle away, since he will be talking nothing but rubbish, and Malvolio is told to make some excuse for Olivia if the visitor is from the Duke Orsino. While Maria and Malvolio are gone Sir Toby enters, drunk, and his niece tries to find out who the 'gentleman' is. But her uncle is too drunk to make sense; when he has stumbled off Olivia sends Feste to look after him.

Malvolio returns and informs Olivia that the young man insists on speaking to her. He will accept no excuses. Olivia asks what sort of man he is and is told that he is young and handsome, with a sharp voice. Olivia relents. She will see him but only in the presence of Maria, who is instructed to veil Olivia's face.

Which details prepare the audience for what is to come?

When Cesario (Viola) enters he embarks on his mission with a series of compliments, while cleverly avoiding Olivia's questions about himself. It is clear that Olivia is very interested in this handsome youth, but he will not tell her his message while other people are present. Olivia dismisses Maria and the attendants. Cesario tells Olivia that his message comes from Orsino's heart and

he asks to see her face. When she unveils herself
Cesario is full of admiration, regretting that the owner
of such beauty should be so cruel as to never have
children and thus 'leave the world no copy' (line 246).
Don't worry, replies Olivia, I will leave an account of
my beauty in writing when I die; every respect of it will
be written down and 'copied'.

In spite of Cesario's affirmation that Orsino truly loves
her, Olivia says she cannot love him in return, despite
all his virtues. He must not continue his suit. Yet if
Cesario would like to return, Olivia will be happy to see
him. She tries to pay him, but Cesario proudly declines
to accept the gold he is offered and leaves.

*The audience
becomes aware of
Olivia's love for
Cesario in the last
part of the scene.*

By now utterly infatuated with Cesario, Olivia recalls
Malvolio and tells him to follow the messenger with a
ring which she claims he has left behind. She asks
Malvolio to tell Cesario that if he returns tomorrow she
will provide more reasons for her refusal of the duke.

At the close of the scene Olivia has fallen in love with
Cesario, the duke's go-between. The ring is a ruse to
make him return.

COMMENT

Feste's attempt to prove Olivia is a fool (lines 55–70) by
mocking her state of mourning anticipates her
behaviour later in the scene.

Olivia provides us with a description of Malvolio's
character (lines 89–93) which is meant to stick in our
minds. He is depicted as an enemy of pleasure and wit
who takes himself and everybody else too seriously.
This prepares the audience for the trick that will be
played on him later.

Olivia is clearly intelligent – she appreciates the
punning (see Literary Terms) paradoxical wit of the
clown and her characterisation of Malvolio is very
accurate – yet indirectly we find out about her capacity

for self-deception in the rapid way she forgets her vows and allows herself to become so attracted to Cesario.

The conversation between Olivia and Cesario starts off in prose and moves to the poetic form of blank verse (see Literary Terms) to emphasise the dialogue's focus on the subject of love.

When Cesario tells Olivia that Orsino loves her 'with adoration, fertile tears, With groans that thunder love, with sighs of fire' (lines 259–60) he is using an exaggerated form of language known as hyperbole (see Literary Terms) which is common to love poetry. Perhaps there is an element of Viola's own feelings for Orsino here, and in the 'willow cabin' speech (lines 272–80).

In spite of all his qualities, Olivia cannot love Orsino (lines 261–6), yet she is amazed at how quickly she has fallen for Cesario (line 299). The irrational nature of love is a major theme of the play.

At the end of Act I Orsino loves Olivia who loves Cesario (Viola) who secretly loves Orsino. This complexity provides the impetus for the rest of the plot and its resolution. It creates a basic dramatic irony (see Literary Terms) in which the audience knows more than the characters.

GLOSSARY	**fear no colours** fear no foe
	lenten thin, weak
	let summer bear it out let the warm weather make it bearable
	barren stupid
	zanies assistants, imitators
	bird bolts blunt arrows
	pia mater brain
	I am very compatible, even to the least sinister usage 'I am sensitive to the least incivility'
	usurp myself impersonate myself (a paradoxical joke)
	such a one I was this present 'this *was* what I was *now*' (Olivia humorously pretends to unveil a portrait of herself)

A *Identify the speaker.*

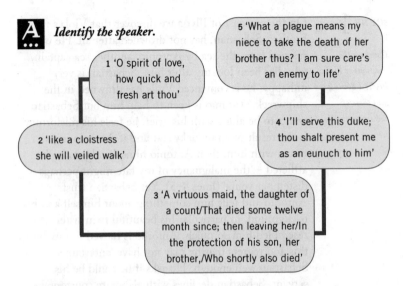

1 'O spirit of love, how quick and fresh art thou'

2 'like a cloistress she will veiled walk'

3 'A virtuous maid, the daughter of a count/That died some twelve month since; then leaving her/In the protection of his son, her brother,/Who shortly also died'

4 'I'll serve this duke; thou shalt present me as an eunuch to him'

5 'What a plague means my niece to take the death of her brother thus? I am sure care's an enemy to life'

Identify the person 'to whom' this comment refers.

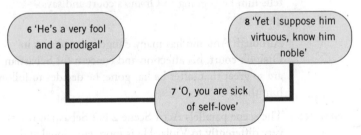

6 'He's a very fool and a prodigal'

7 'O, you are sick of self-love'

8 'Yet I suppose him virtuous, know him noble'

Check your answers on page 87.

B *Consider these issues.*

a How Shakespeare develops the character of Orsino as an 'extravagant, self-indulgent man'.

b The way the characters are grouped and a parallel story (sub-plot – see Literary Terms) is prepared.

c The attitudes towards love which emerge.

d The effect of the dramatic irony (see Literary Terms).

ACT II

SCENE 1

Compare the reactions of Viola in Act I Scene 2 and those of Sebastian in this scene.

On the seacoast of Illyria we discover that Viola's twin brother, Sebastian, has not drowned after all. He was rescued from the sea by Antonio, another sea captain, who has been looking after him. Sebastian is very unhappy; he is convinced Viola has drowned in the shipwreck. Antonio is keen to help him but Sebastian wants to be alone with his grief: he feels his misfortune is the result of an unlucky star and if Antonio joins forces with him, then Antonio himself might also be afflicted – 'the malignancy of my fate might perhaps distemper yours' (lines 4–5). Yet Sebastian trusts Antonio and tells him something about himself and his background, in particular his beautiful twin sister who resembled him so much. Antonio is moved to pity by this and regrets that he may not have 'entertained' Sebastian well enough. He asks if he could be his servant. Sebastian declines with elaborate courtesy; he cannot stand being a burden to Antonio any longer. He tells him he is going to Orsino's court and says goodbye.

Although Antonio has many dangerous enemies in Orsino's court, his affection and concern for Sebastian are so great that, after he has gone, he decides to follow him there.

COMMENT   The scene parallels Act I Scene 2 but Sebastian reacts very differently to Viola. He is more emotional and impulsive, as we will see later on in the play, and is sure Viola has drowned.

The appearance of Sebastian, whom the now disguised Viola believed drowned, anticipates the comic complications of mistaken identity in Act V; he will be mistaken for Cesario (Viola), and Viola (as Cesario) will be mistaken for Sebastian. Sebastian is an attractive figure who commands respect and love reflected in Antonio's decision to follow him.

GLOSSARY   **distemper** infect
            my determinate ... extravagancy 'my only plan of travel is to
              have no plan'
            in an hour at the same time
            If you ... servant Let me be your servant or I shall die of grief at
              losing you
            manners of my mother womanly readiness to weep

SCENE 2   Cesario (Viola) is followed by Malvolio who asks him if
             he is the same person who was recently with the
             Countess Olivia. Cesario replies that he is, and
             Malvolio proffers the ring which he has been told to
             return to the youth. Malvolio tells him sarcastically that
             he would have been spared the trouble of returning it to
             Cesario if Cesario had not been so forgetful. With great
             contempt Malvolio relates what Olivia wishes Cesario
             to tell Orsino. He is to make it clear that she will have
             nothing to do with the duke. Cesario must never return
             with any more of Orsino's messages, except if it be to
             report to Olivia how Orsino took this rejection.

             Cesario is put off by Malvolio's arrogant and scornful
             manner, and refuses the ring: 'I'll none of it' (line 22).
             The outraged Malvolio flings the ring to the ground
             and departs.

             Alone on the stage, Viola reflects on what has
             happened. Since she certainly left no ring with Olivia,
             she fears that her appearance ('outside') has 'charm'd'
             the countess. She is appalled to remember the details of
             her interview with Olivia, how she spoke in fits and
             starts, her vague distracted manner. All the evidence
             points her to the conclusion that Olivia has fallen in
             love with 'Cesario'. Obviously sending the 'churlish'
             Malvolio with the ring was a trick to lure the messenger
             back.

             Viola feels pity for Olivia. The lady might just as well
             'love a dream' as a woman disguised as a man. Disguise

The fact that we have just met Sebastian makes us confident that 'time' will indeed provide a solution.

is a 'wickedness', the work of the devil, and Viola laments how easy it is for attractive but dishonest suitors to impress women's 'waxen hearts'. Viola is a woman, like Olivia, and women are frail and impressionable. Finally, she expresses the terribly complex situation which has arisen: Viola loves Orsino, her master, as much as he loves Olivia; Olivia mistakenly dotes on Cesario, who is really a woman, Viola. She cannot think of a solution. She calls on time to unravel this 'hard' knot and the scene ends.

COMMENT

This scene continues the action which started at the end of Act I.

Malvolio's character is even more explicitly arrogant and scornful here and part of the purpose is to bring this out so that the audience will be pleased when the trick is played on him. He despises anyone who is not above him socially.

Viola's soliloquy (see Literary Terms) is important. It allows her to express her feelings directly to the audience and to sum up the basic problem which the rest of the play has to resolve.

GLOSSARY

desperate assurance hopeless certainty
pregnant enemy the devil
proper false handsome and deceitful men
fadge turn out
monster both 'man' and 'woman'
desperate hopeless
thriftless unprofitable

SCENE 3

Look at the different elements which contribute to the comedy of this scene.

Late at night in Olivia's house Sir Toby Belch and Sir Andrew Aguecheek are having a drinking session. Their drunken conversation consists at first of a wildly absurd piece of reasoning prompted by Sir Toby, in which he tries to justify their late hours. To be up after midnight, he says, is to be up early 'and *dilucolo surgere,* thou know'st' (lines 2–3) – (to rise early is very healthy). Sir Toby pursues the argument until the 'scholar' Sir Andrew concludes that life 'consists of eating and drinking' (lines 11–12). So let us eat and drink, agrees Sir Toby, calling Maria for some more wine.

Feste, the clown, is also up late and he enters, adding to the scene of broad comedy his own brand of word-play and nonsense. Sir Andrew is delighted with the clown's fooling, and knowing he has a sweet voice asks him to sing. Sir Toby requests a love song.

Feste sings a song, 'O Mistress Mine', that urges young lovers to live for the moment and not delay their lovemaking; the future is always uncertain and youth does not last. These sentiments and Feste's beautiful voice please Sir Toby and Sir Andrew greatly. After some more verbal knockabout, the three decide to sing together a catch, a piece of music where one part follows another. 'I am dog at a catch' (lines 62–3), cries Sir Andrew happily. They make a terrible sound and Maria rushes in to complain at their 'caterwauling'. If Olivia is woken up by the noise she will have Malvolio throw them out of the house.

What does Malvolio look like when he arrives to break up the party?

Maria's entreaties are ignored by the revellers who are too drunk to take anything or anybody seriously. Sir Toby dubs Malvolio a 'Peg-a-Ramsey', that is, a spoil-sport, and just as he begins a new song, 'On the Twelfth Day of December', an indignant Malvolio appears.

Does Malvolio's speech reflect his character? How?

Olivia's steward scolds them for their lack of manners and respect for others, and for making a vulgar ale-house out of his mistress's home. He has been instructed by Olivia to tell Sir Toby that although he is her relative, she cannot tolerate his disorderly ways. If he will not stop this rowdiness he must leave at once. Malvolio is roundly mocked for this by Sir Toby and

Feste, who relentlessly continue their singing. They think that Malvolio's high-handed sanctimonious manner is intolerable. Before he goes off, the scandalised steward assures Maria that he will be reporting her part in the unruliness to her mistress. Maria responds to his parting shot with scorn – 'Go shake your ears' (line 124) – and proposes a plan to make the pompous Malvolio look a fool.

She reveals that she will forge a love letter in Olivia's handwriting, which is often mistaken for her's, and this letter will contain an admiring description of Malvolio, 'the colour of his beard, the shape of his leg, the manner of his gait, the expressure of his eye, forehead, and complexion' (lines 156–8). Malvolio will find it and foolishly believe that Olivia is in love with him. Maria knows she can accomplish the trick and she suggests that the two knights spy on Malvolio 'where he shall find the letter' (lines 174–5) to watch how he interprets it.

Sir Toby and Sir Andrew are delighted at the prospect of this opportunity to bring down Malvolio. They think Maria is an excellent woman and she certainly 'adores' Sir Toby, who once more encourages Sir Andrew to believe he will have Olivia. Deciding it is too late to go to bed, Sir Toby leads Sir Andrew off in search of more wine.

COMMENT

Summarise the revellers' objections to Malvolio.

The sub-plot now develops and Malvolio is built up further as a thoroughly unsympathetic character.

We are given a statement of the basic conflict between Sir Toby's values and those of Malvolio: 'Dost thou think, because thou art virtuous, there shall be no more cake and ale?' (lines 114–15). Sir Toby and his friends stand for a tolerant pleasure-loving view of life, and Malvolio stands for the puritanical denial of pleasure.

We learn that Sir Toby is not just an ordinary wise-cracking drunkard: he is a man of some wit and learning, which comes through even though he is drunk. His characteristic form of wit is the quibble – playing on words which are ambiguous.

Connections are made between past and future events in Sir Andrew's offer to challenge Malvolio and in Maria's reference to Olivia's state of mind after she has just seen Cesario. In this way Shakespeare maintains dramatic credibility in the action.

Maria reveals her plan to get even with Malvolio and gives her reasons quite explicitly (line 146 onwards). Her analysis of Malvolio's psychology is penetrating. Shakespeare is presenting a viewpoint which he wants the audience to share while at the same time demonstrating Maria's sharpness of mind.

The clown's song is a point of seriousness in the scene. It announces the play's main theme of love and contrasts with the raucous part-songs which, in turn, are contrasted by the music of the following scene featuring the Duke Orsino and Viola.

GLOSSARY	**stoup** large drinking vessel
	picture of 'we three' popular inn sign depicting two fools, or two asses, the caption hence including the spectator
	breast singing voice
	coziers cobblers
	Sneck up! Be hanged!
	rub your chain with crumbs polish your stewards chain
	gull him into a nayword trick him so that his name is synonymous with 'fool'
	time-pleaser time-server
	cons state without book memorises official jargon
	Penthesilea the Queen of the Amazons

SCENE 4

*This is the first
time we see Viola
and Orsino
together after her
confession that she
loves him (Act I
Scene 4).*

Duke Orsino is with his courtiers in his palace. He calls
for music to be played. He tells Cesario that he would
particularly like to hear a song that was performed
during the previous evening; 'That old and antic song'
(line 3) seemed to soothe his emotions far more than
any of the superficial songs of the present time. Curio is
sent to bring Feste, the clown, to sing and while they
are waiting the duke talks to Cesario against a
background of the old tune played by the musicians.

The duke tells Cesario to remember him if he should
ever fall in love. For he, Orsino, is the typical true lover,
lively and playful in all emotions except when he has in
mind the 'constant image' of his beloved. Cesario hints
that he himself already knows something about what it
means to love and when Orsino asks him if he has ever
been in love, Cesario cautiously admits that he has. The
duke becomes curious about the woman who has
attracted him. He questions the youth about what she is
like, her appearance and age.

Cesario says that the woman is very like Orsino, both in
temperament and age. Orsino is scornful: this woman is
therefore unworthy of Cesario and certainly too old. A
woman should take an older man, he advises, because
women by their nature become emotionally mature
earlier than men and an older man is more likely to
satisfy their needs. We young men may think highly of
ourselves in love, he says, but our emotions are unstable,
'more giddy and unfirm' (line 33), more easily worn out
than those of women. Orsino recommends Cesario find
himself a virgin in the first bloom of youthful beauty.
She will keep his love alive for longer. Cesario agrees.

Curio returns with Feste and Orsino instructs the
clown to sing the song. He tells Cesario to note that
the song is 'old and plain' (line 43) and used to be sung
by both old women and carefree young maids. The
simple truth of its theme is the innocence of love.

Feste, the clown, draws attention to Orsino's changeable nature (lines 73–4) and this quality influences the duke's subsequent reflections on love.

The lover in this melancholy song is a young man whose heart has been broken by a 'fair cruel maid' (line 54). He wishes to die and be buried without friends or other mourners so that no one will know where his bones are laid, 'O where/Sad true lover never find my grave,/To weep there' (lines 64–6). Clearly the deep sadness of the song reflects the duke's mood; he is pleased with Feste's performance and pays him for it.

Everybody except the duke and Cesario leave and Orsino tells him that he must return to Olivia and convince her that his love for her is truly noble. He is not impressed by Olivia's wealth and possessions – his soul loves her for what nature has made her, 'that miracle and queen of gems' (line 86), her beauty. And what, asks Cesario, if she cannot love you? Orsino replies that he will not be refused.

Cesario tells Orsino that he must accept her refusal. After all, if the duke were the object of some lady's passion, and he did not love her in return, he would be forced to tell her and expect her to accept it. Orsino does not believe that women can love as passionately as men. He thinks women simply do not have the physical capacity to retain deep feeling; they quickly become sick of love by being too greedy for it in the first place. Orsino's love, by comparison, is 'as hungry as the sea' (line 101) and like the deep ocean can absorb far more. He is adamant that there is no comparison between the love any woman could feel for him and the feelings he has for Olivia.

Cesario, who of course is really Viola and loves Orsino, replies that he knows only too well how much women are able to love men. Their hearts, he says, are as 'true' as 'we' men. He knows this because his father had a daughter who loved a man quite as much as he might love Orsino if he, Cesario, were a woman. Orsino is intrigued by this and asks what happened to the girl. She 'never told her love' (line 111), recounts Cesario, but pined away concealing her feelings from her beloved, so intensely that her concealed love consumed all her youth. He tells Orsino that 'we' men may talk a lot about our feelings, but we profess more than we actually feel. And, Orsino asks, did your sister die of her love? Cesario answers with a riddle: 'I am all the daughters of my father's house,/And all the brothers too' (lines 120–1). On this mysterious note the scene ends. Orsino dispatches Cesario to Olivia. He is to tell her that the duke's love cannot be denied.

COMMENT This scene provides a strong contrast to the previous one and the change of mood is established as much by music – the 'caterwauling' in Olivia's house and the 'old and antic' song in Orsino's as by the seriousness of the conversation between Orsino and Cesario.

Viola's disguise has created a strong dramatic irony: read the scene from Orsino's point of view and then from the audience's.

The fact that Feste sings a song in both locations provides continuity and also points to Feste's independence, the 'allowed fool' who is free to move and speak where he will.

We are more interested in Viola's emotions here than in Orsino's. A tension is created between her 'fictional' role as the man, Cesario, and the real feelings she tries to express indirectly as a woman who is secretly in love with Orsino. The true pathos (see Literary Terms) of Viola's situation is given, yet this is qualified by the irony created by Orsino's ignorance of 'Cesario's' true identity and the way Shakespeare is developing an increasingly intimate relationship between them.

Look at the way the scene is constructed. The two dialogues between Orsino and Cesario are separated by Feste's song, the theme of which is unrequited love and which reflects the emotional situation of both Orsino and Viola.

The ending of the scene moves the plot on further, anticipating another meeting between Olivia and Cesario (Viola).

GLOSSARY

recollected terms learned phrases

wears she to him adapts to him

hold the bent stand the strain

silly sooth simple truth

changeable taffeta changing lights and colours

giddily indifferently, lightly

pranks adorns

motion emotion

Our shows are more than will what we show is greater than our feelings

SCENE 5

In Olivia's garden Sir Toby, Sir Andrew and one of her servants, Fabian, meet together in anticipation of the trick they are playing on Malvolio. Fabian is keen to watch this 'sport' since he also has a grudge against the sanctimonious puritan: Malvolio has reported him to Olivia for bear baiting, a popular sport of the Elizabethans. Sir Toby tells him that they will soon be turning Malvolio into an angry, beaten bear himself.

Soon Maria arrives with the 'bait', the forged letter, and she tells them to hide themselves in the 'box-tree'. The self-regarding Malvolio is approaching and Maria drops the letter on the path where he will find it easily. Malvolio will be caught by having his vanity tickled, she assures them before she leaves.

Malvolio finds the letter when his ludicrous ambitions and pretensions are at their height.

Malvolio enters and he is a character who is ripe for mockery. He is engrossed in thoughts of Olivia and the possibility that she might love him. Did not Maria once tell him that his mistress admired him? And has not Olivia herself admitted that if she should ever fall in love again, it would be with someone very like Malvolio? He knows that she respects him far more than any of her other servants.

To the indignation of the eavesdroppers, Malvolio proceeds to fantasise about being married to Olivia, being 'Count Malvolio'. After all, there has been an instance when a noble lady married one of her servants. Malvolio has no difficulty picturing himself as a loving husband, dressed in velvet, surrounded by servants who would defer to his authoritative manner. And it would be a special pleasure to be able to summon Sir Toby Belch and remind him that he now has the right to give him orders. He would instruct Olivia's uncle to give up his drunkenness and tell him that he is wasting too much time with a foolish knight, 'One Sir Andrew' (line 80).

Imagine the gestures and expressions of Malvolio as he reads the letter.

Then Malvolio catches sight of the letter. He picks it up and begins to read it out loud, utterly convinced it is in Olivia's handwriting. The phrases used in the letter are typical of Olivia and the note has her stamp, so it must be from her. There is a love poem inside and the first verse says that only God knows the man whom the writer loves and she must tell no one who it is. If only this person were Malvolio! The second verse prompts him to believe it is indeed him whom she loves because Olivia writes 'I may command where I adore' (line 106). He, after all, is her steward and she may command him:

'I serve her, she is my lady' (line 117). The first part is all quite logical, but what of the letters M.O.A.I. which end the poem? Malvolio soon takes them to signify him, since all the letters are in his name.

Malvolio then finds a prose letter enclosed with the poem. It is this letter that finally convinces him that Olivia loves him. The letter says that if it should by chance fall into her beloved's hands, then he should consider the fact that the woman who loves him is, through fate, socially his superior. He should not be afraid of this 'greatness' – 'Some are born great, some achieve greatness, and some have greatness thrust upon 'em' (lines 145–6). The author of the letter writes that Fate calls on him to take the initiative for he is being made a very generous offer. He should be bold, cast off his usual clothes and start wearing yellow stockings and cross garters. He should be rude to servants and go about talking of important, high-flown subjects. Unless he does all these things he will still be thought of as a mere steward, a servant who is 'not worthy to touch Fortune's fingers' (lines 156–7). The letter is signed 'The Fortunate-Unhappy'.

Yellow stockings and cross garters would have been considered laughably unfashionable by the Elizabethan audience.

Malvolio is overjoyed after reading this letter. He tells himself he will do all that has been 'commended'. He will be 'proud', he will treat Sir Toby with contempt, he will have nothing to do with low-born acquaintance, he will be exactly the man described in the letter. For it is as clear as daylight that Olivia wrote it, and nothing makes this plainer than the reference to yellow stockings and cross garters, for Olivia has recently admired his stockings and obviously wants him to continue the habit.

A postscript to the letter which Malvolio reads out contains more encouragement. It says that by now he must surely realise who the writer is and, if he is prepared to love her, he should show this by smiling in her presence, smiling all the time.

After Malvolio exits, Sir Toby, Sir Andrew and Fabian emerge from their hiding place and soon Maria returns to join them. They are all very pleased with the trick which she has played on Malvolio. Sir Toby especially is full of admiration and claims he would marry her and 'ask no other dowry ... but such another jest' (lines 184–5). He tells Maria that with this demonstration of her cleverness she has completely conquered him. The letter has put Malvolio 'in such a dream' (line 193) that when he wakes up to reality he will go mad. Maria tells them that if they want to see the 'fruits of the sport' (line 197) they must watch for Malvolio's next encounter with Olivia. He is sure to appear in yellow stockings (a colour she hates) and cross garters ('a fashion she detests' – line 200). And Malvolio's endless smiling is bound to make the melancholic Olivia extremely annoyed.

The hoaxers all go off, keenly looking forward to Malvolio's humiliation.

COMMENT   This scene provides another strong contrast and takes us back again into the comic sub-plot, the gulling of Malvolio. We meet a new character, Fabian, who offers a further reason for the attack on Malvolio's vanity and sanctimoniousness: the steward has reported him for bear baiting, a sport much disapproved of by Puritans.

At the entrance of Malvolio we find him already absorbed in his ambitious fantasies, so his conceit makes him an easy target for the tricksters. And it is this conceit, combined with his egotistical pretensions, which makes the trick possible.

The dramatic convention of soliloquy (see Literary

Terms), where a character speaks his thoughts alone, is exploited to full comic effect here.

The letter is signed with a typical Elizabethan oxymoron (see Literary Terms) – a paradox that combines one idea with its opposite.

Maria has obviously conceived the letter knowing very well what her mistress dislikes, and she clearly understands Malvolio's character as well in the way the letter plays upon his weaknesses.

The audience is made to anticipate future events in this scene, in particular through the expectation of an hilarious encounter between Malvolio and Olivia (Act III Scene 4).

GLOSSARY   **boiled to death with melancholy** (a joke) – melancholy was considered a cold humour

contemplative idiot empty fool

Look how imagination blows him look how his thoughts swell him up (in self-importance)

demure travel of regard grave survey of those present

fustian high-flown language

formal capacity normal reasoning

point-device the very man follow the advice in every detail

strange aloof

A Identify the speaker.

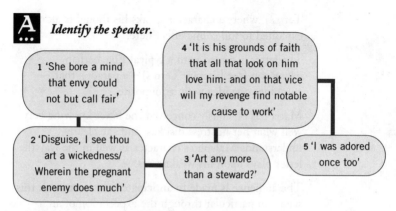

1 'She bore a mind that envy could not but call fair'

2 'Disguise, I see thou art a wickedness/ Wherein the pregnant enemy does much'

3 'Art any more than a steward?'

4 'It is his grounds of faith that all that look on him love him: and on that vice will my revenge find notable cause to work'

5 'I was adored once too'

Identify the person 'to whom' this comment refers.

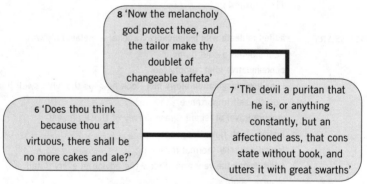

8 'Now the melancholy god protect thee, and the tailor make thy doublet of changeable taffeta'

6 'Does thou think because thou art virtuous, there shall be no more cakes and ale?'

7 'The devil a puritan that he is, or anything constantly, but an affectioned ass, that cons state without book, and utters it with great swarths'

Check your answers on page 87.

B Consider these issues.

a How Shakespeare prepares us for the part which mistaken identities will play in the plot.

b The way Malvolio's character is built up through his actions and speech, and what is said about him.

c How Shakespeare determines the audience's attitude towards Malvolio.

d The situation Viola finds herself in and the representation of Orsino's unconscious interest in her.

e The role of disguise and the different aspects of outer versus inner reality, illusion and truth.

ACT III

Still in disguise as Cesario, Viola has once more come to Olivia's house with Orsino's entreaties of love. In the garden she meets Feste, the clown, who is playing on the pipe and drum. They indulge in some light-hearted witty conversation until Cesario points out that people who play so cleverly with words, as Feste does, may soon give them lewd double meanings. He asks Feste if he is Olivia's fool and the jester replies that he is not: 'She will keep no fool, sir, till she be married' (lines 33–4). Rather, he is her 'corrupter of words' (line 37).

Feste's wit provides a lively start to Act III.

Feste treats Cesario with careful deference while at the same time demonstrating that he is his equal in wit. And Cesario is pleased with this diversion before the serious business which he has come to perform; he pays the clown who goes inside to announce his presence.

While waiting Cesario reflects on the role of the fool, which to perform well requires intelligence and sensitivity. The fool must be aware of the mood and social status of each person he makes fun of, measuring his wit to fit the occasion and not just let his jokes fly anywhere. To be a good fool, concludes Cesario, is as difficult as 'a wise man's art' (line 67).

At this point Sir Toby and Sir Andrew enter. The two knights are terribly impressed by Cesario's manners, and Sir Andrew in particular is struck by his courtly language: 'That youth's a rare courtier' (line 88) he observes.

When Olivia arrives she orders all the others to leave so that she can be alone with Cesario. Straightaway she asks for his hand, but he keeps his distance, reminding her that he is her servant because, being the servant of Orsino, who is her servant in love, he, Cesario, is therefore her servant. Olivia is dismissive of such complicated reasoning and wishes that Orsino thought nothing of her. She does not want to speak of the duke.

Her thoughts are all on Cesario and she would much
prefer it if he had come to woo her for himself.

*Olivia's response
to Cesario reveals
she is as
changeable in love
as Orsino.*

She then confesses that she sent Malvolio with the ring
simply as an excuse to make him return to her. She is
unhappy and wants Cesario to think well of her, even
though she thinks he must despise her for being so
frank with her feelings. All Cesario can say is that he
pities her. That at least is close to love, ventures Olivia.
Cesario disagrees: we often pity our enemies, he says.
Olivia cannot conceal her disappointment at being
rejected by Cesario, yet she assures him that she will
not pursue the subject further. Whoever marries
Cesario will certainly be marrying a 'proper man' (line
135) she says.

*Viola must break
all contact with
Olivia if the
disguise is to
remain
undetected.*

As Cesario prepares to leave he asks Olivia one last
time if she has any message for Duke Orsino. Olivia
pleads with him to stay and tell her what he thinks of
her. After a guarded and ambiguous exchange in which
both confess they are not what they appear to be, Olivia
breaks into an impassioned declaration of her love for
Cesario. No woman ever has or ever will conquer my
heart, Cesario informs her, and bids her farewell. Olivia
begs him to come again in the hope that one day he
may indeed be able to love her.

COMMENT   This scene continues the events of ACT II Scene 4 in which Orsino sent Cesario to Olivia. The scenes of the main romantic plot alternate with those of the sub-plot (see Literary Terms). By starting this scene with some of the comic characters, Shakespeare begins to bring the two plots together.

Cesario's style of speaking impresses Sir Andrew. Later the knight's jealousy will be fuelled by this and give rise to the pretend duel between the two (Act III Scene 4).

The clown gives a good demonstration of his wit, his ability to make puns (see Literary Terms) and to be Olivia's 'corrupter of words' (line 37). Viola's appreciation (lines 61–9) complements Olivia's remark (Act I Scene 5, lines 93–4): the clown's humour contains no 'slander'.

The dialogue (lines 140–6) functions to underline the complications which the disguise has caused: both Cesario and Olivia are 'not what they are' – Cesario is really a woman; Olivia thinks she is in love with a man.

The final speeches of the scene are in rhyming couplets (see Literary Terms) which serve to distance us from the turbulent emotions being expressed and underscore the irony of the situation.

GLOSSARY   **dally nicely** play subtly
wanton equivocal, licentious
and thou pass upon me If you make me the butt of your jokes
coster explain
and like the haggard probably '*not* like the haggard'
folly-fall'n, quite taint their wits having fallen into folly, betray their intelligence
Taste your legs try your legs
pregnant and vouchsafed ear receptive and kindly granted ear
hard construction adverse interpretation
grize step
clause premise

SCENE *2*

Sir Andrew, Sir Toby and Fabian are in Olivia's house discussing Sir Andrew's attempt to win the affections of Olivia. He has become more and more frustrated with his lack of progress and wants to return to his home. He believes that Olivia cares more for the 'Count's serving-man' (line 5), Cesario, than she does for him. Sir Andrew has seen them together in the orchard, and it was clear that Olivia is in love with the youth from the way she behaved. Fabian tells him that she showed 'favour' to Cesario just to make Sir Andrew jealous. What Olivia wanted was for Sir Andrew to march up to them and insult Cesario, and then he 'should have banged the youth into a dumbness' (line 21). As it is, the knight has lost a perfect opportunity to demonstrate his valour. He is therefore in her low opinion, where he must 'hang like an icicle on a Dutchman's beard' (lines 25–6) unless he redeems himself by some act of courage or strategy ('policy').

Sir Toby and Fabian create some more comic mischief: this time at the expense of Sir Andrew.

Sir Andrew decides to do something courageous – 'policy' he associates with scheming politicians – and Sir Toby suggests he challenge Cesario to a duel, sending him off to write the challenge and giving him some advice on what to say.

When the foolish Aguecheek has gone, Sir Toby and Fabian laugh at this new practical joke they are playing. They are certain that neither Sir Andrew, who is a coward, nor Cesario, who is peaceable, will ever come to fight one another.

Maria arrives to inform them that Malvolio is obeying 'every point of the letter' (line 74). He has donned a pair of yellow stockings and 'does smile his face into more lines than is in the new map with the augmentation of the Indies' (lines 75–7). She leads them off the stage to enjoy the absurd result of their practical joke.

COMMENT   The purpose of this short scene is chiefly to move the
sub-plot (see Literary Terms) along.

We learn more of Sir Andrew's stupidity from the fact
that he continues to believe he has a chance with Olivia
and allows himself to be duped by Fabian and Sir Toby,
the latter still interested in his money.

To complement this new practical joke we are given a
glimpse of Malvolio's behaviour with Olivia, making
two dupes.

Sir Andrew is foolish, but Malvolio is arrogant to
believe that Olivia can love him.

GLOSSARY   **prove it legitimate** show it is valid
dormouse valour sleeping courage
Brownist puritan (after Robert Brown – the reformer)
with ... ink the freedom permitted by writing
bed of Ware a famous bedstead of exceptional size
cubiculo little bedroom
a dear mannikin to you a puppet whom you enjoy manipulating
Anatomy body (corpse)
the youngest wren of nine smallest of small birds
spleen laughter
impossible passages of grossness improbabilities

SCENE 3   Viola's twin brother, Sebastian, and Antonio the sea
captain, walk in the street near Orsino's palace.

Antonio is shown   Antonio has done what he said he would do (Act II
as a brave and   Scene 1) and followed Sebastian into Illyria. He tells
honest character.   Sebastian that he could not let him wander alone in a
strange country: his affection and concern overcame
any anxieties he had about his own safety. Antonio
relates that he was once in a sea-fight against the duke's
ships. He played such a prominent part in this battle
that if he were caught he would probably be put to
death.

The scene prepares
later complications
of mistaken
identity. Sebastian is full of gratitude for the risk Antonio has
taken, and Antonio tells him that it would be best if he
went undercover while Sebastian does some sightseeing.
He hands Sebastian a purse containing money and they
agree to meet later at an inn called The Elephant.

COMMENT There is a strong bond of friendship between the two
men – Antonio's loyalty and concern, and Sebastian's
gratitude, are emphasised for a particular dramatic
purpose which will become apparent later in the play.

The gift of money will feature in the plot when Viola,
disguised as Cesario, is mistaken by Antonio for
Sebastian.

GLOSSARY **jealousy** anxiety
skilless in unacquainted with
uncurrent pay worthless payment
for traffic's sake for the sake of trade
bespeak our diet i.e. arrange for our meals
your store ... idle markets i.e. you don't have enough money for
trivial purchases

SCENE 4 Olivia is in her garden anxiously expecting to entertain
Cesario, who she has invited to visit her. She wonders
where Malvolio is. His serious and polite manner would
soothe her disturbed emotions. Maria informs her that
Malvolio is on his way to see her, but warns her
mistress that he has become 'very strange' (line 8) and is
probably possessed by the devil.

With a foolish smile on his face, Malvolio enters. Olivia
is disconcerted. Her steward has shed his normally dark
clothes and is wearing yellow stockings. He is far from
the 'sad and civil' (line 5) Malvolio she is used to,
having transformed himself into the ludicrous parody of
a fawning courtier, smiling inanely and blowing her
kisses, and making suggestive references to what he
believes to be her feelings towards him. He pays no

attention to her expressions of surprise and confusion and continues to quote various lines from the forged letter. Olivia tries to get some sense out of him – what is this talk about 'greatness'? – but Malvolio continues to ramble on, to such a degree of absurdity that Olivia concludes he is suffering from some kind of 'midsummer madness' (line 55).

Malvolio has no idea he has been made to look such a fool.

The arrival of Cesario is announced and before she goes off to see him Olivia instructs Maria to take charge of the deranged Malvolio. She asks for other members of her household to look after him too, including Sir Toby.

Left alone on the stage, Malvolio recalls what the letter said concerning how he must treat Sir Toby ('be opposite with a kinsman' – line 69) and when the knight enters, accompanied by Fabian and Maria, he is rude to them all. Eventually they are driven to exasperation by Malvolio's behaviour. After he has left they plan to have him locked up in a dark room, the customary place for Elizabethan lunatics. Sir Toby reminds them that Olivia already thinks Malvolio is mad, so they can carry their joke a little further, 'for our pleasure and his penance' (lines 138–9).

At this point another object of mockery enters. Sir Andrew Aguecheek is clutching the challenge he has just written to Cesario. He is very proud of this piece of writing and Sir Toby reads it out loud. The absurd language, full of wooden and obscure phrases, is ironically admired by Fabian, and Sir Toby says he will personally deliver the challenge himself. Maria informs them that Cesario is at present with Olivia, so this would be an excellent time to hand it over.

Sir Toby advises Sir Andrew to approach Cesario from behind, with his sword drawn and swearing horribly. This will make the knight look very tough and manly, far more than any actual deed of courage. Sir Andrew goes off to do battle with Cesario.

Aware that such an absurdly phrased challenge would not frighten the well-bred Cesario, but simply make him think it came from an illiterate idiot, Sir Toby decides to deliver the challenge verbally. He will play off Aguecheek and Cesario against one another, making each so frightened 'that they will kill one another by the look, like cockatrices' (lines 196–7). Just as the jokers are leaving the stage, Olivia enters with Cesario. Sir Toby decides to leave them together for a while to give him time to think up 'some horrid message for a challenge' (lines 201–2).

A short conversation follows in which Olivia continues to 'woo' Cesario, who steadfastly declares his master's suit. Olivia gives him a jewelled brooch containing a miniature portrait of herself, and after telling him to return to her the next day, she leaves.

The manipulative aspects of Sir Toby's character are prominent in this scene.

Sir Toby and Fabian then return and Sir Toby tells Cesario to prepare to defend himself, for his 'interceptor', Sir Andrew, is waiting for him in the orchard. He must draw his sword quickly for Sir Andrew is a 'skillful, and deadly' (line 227) opponent.

Cesario can think of no man who might want to fight him; he has offended no one. Sir Toby proceeds to paint a picture of Sir Andrew as a fearsome fighter, a 'devil' who has killed three men already in private disputes. Cesario becomes very alarmed and makes to return to Olivia's house to seek protection, but Sir Toby urges him on to fight – 'strip your sword stark naked' (line 254).

Cesario implores Sir Toby to go to this knight and discover what offence he has given and the knight exits, pretending to do this, leaving the frightened courtier in the charge of Fabian. Fabian leads him off to 'the most skillful, bloody and fatal opposite that you could possibly have found in any part of Illyria' (lines 270–2).

Sir Toby and Sir Andrew enter, and Aguecheek is soon reduced to terror by Sir Toby's description of Cesario's ferocity. He offers to give Cesario his horse 'Capilet' in order to pacify him, and when Cesario returns the two 'opponents' are provoked to draw their swords.

The unexpected entrance of Antonio points towards the uniting of Viola and Sebastian in Act V.

Suddenly, Antonio enters. He sees Cesario and mistakenly believes it is his friend, Sebastian, Viola's twin brother. He calls on Sir Andrew to put up his sword, unless he wants to fight Antonio. Just as Sir Toby draws *his* sword and prepares to fight Antonio, a troop of officers arrive on the scene. They have come for Antonio. He has been recognised in the street and Orsino has sent them to arrest him.

Antonio is a decent, sincere man whose indignation is based on the fact of Viola's disguise - he feels he has been misled by Sebastian's appearance of nobility (dramtic irony).

Antonio appeals to Cesario for help and asks him for the return of his money. Cesario, who at this point naturally knows nothing of Antonio's mistake, denies he has been given any money by the man. But out of charity he offers to give him some money, since he has shown him such kindness. Antonio is both grieved and angered by what he thinks is the ingratitude of a friend. He tells the crowd that he once rescued this youth from 'the jaws of death' (line 369) and subsequently served him with great devotion. He turns on Cesario and curses him: 'But O how vile an idol proves this god! Thou hast, Sebastian, done good features shame' (lines 374–5). The officers take him away.

When Viola (Cesario) hears the name 'Sebastian' she becomes hopeful that Antonio's mistake reveals the possibility that her brother is still alive. Surely, she thinks, it is possible that Antonio has indeed saved her brother from the shipwreck and because of her disguise has thought she was him. 'For him I imitate' (line 393).

She prays for this to be true and leaves the stage. Sir
Toby and Fabian squeeze out the last drop of fun
from their joke by convincing the foolish Sir Andrew
that Cesario is a coward and has run away. They urge
him to follow the page and 'cuff him soundly' (line
401).

COMMENT   This scene is one of the two longest scenes in the entire
play. It can be divided up into several sections featuring
different groups of characters and exploiting the
mistaken identities and deceptions which Shakespeare
has been preparing in the previous scenes. The deceived
or mistaken characters are Malvolio, Olivia, Viola, Sir
Andrew and Antonio.

When Malvolio enters, the change in his appearance is
very dramatic and very funny. Much of the comedy is
derived from his total confidence that Olivia knows
what he is talking about when he quotes from the
letter. Maria at this point is the only one on the stage
who shares with the audience the truth of the joke.

Note how Sir Toby takes a prominent part in the scene.
He devises some more fun between Sir Andrew and
Cesario, knowing full well that neither will come to any
harm.

Their duel derives its comic irony from the fact that
Olivia is unaware of Sir Andrew's intentions towards
her and has been rejected by Cesario anyway.

An additional absurdity is the entrance of Antonio,
who attempts to defend 'Sebastian' (Viola disguised as
Cesario) and ends up drawing swords with the
pugnacious Sir Toby.

We sense at the end of the scene that the various
elements of the plot's confusions are soon to be
unravelled. Thus when Viola hears her brother's name
it marks a turning point, even though the 'knot' will not

Y

be untied until after Sebastian has been mistaken for Cesario.

GLOSSARY **sad and civil** serious and formal

limed caught

not after my degree not named by my title (i.e. steward)

incredulous or unsafe incredible or undependable

private own company

bawcock fine fellow

More matter for a May morning another subject fit for a May pageant

bum-bailey a bailiff who approaches from behind

cockatrices fabulous serpents that could kill with a glance

Dismount thy tuck Draw your sword

Hob, nob Have or have not

my present such money as I have at present

A ... *Identify the speaker.*

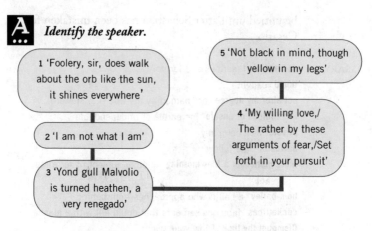

1 'Foolery, sir, does walk about the orb like the sun, it shines everywhere'

2 'I am not what I am'

3 'Yond gull Malvolio is turned heathen, a very renegado'

5 'Not black in mind, though yellow in my legs'

4 'My willing love,/ The rather by these arguments of fear,/Set forth in your pursuit'

Identify the person 'to whom' this comment refers.

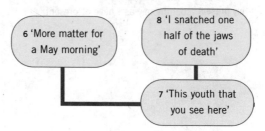

6 'More matter for a May morning'

8 'I snatched one half of the jaws of death'

7 'This youth that you see here'

Check your answers on page 87.

B ... *Consider these issues.*

a How the comic mood of the act is introduced at the start.

b The consequences of Viola's disguise.

c The way Sir Toby and Fabian manipulate both Sir Andrew and Cesario.

d How Shakespeare presents the friendship between Antonio and Sebastian.

e The part mistaken identity and deception play in the final scene, and the way the different groupings of characters are presented.

f How the ending of the act prepares the audience for a resolution which will feature Sebastian.

ACT IV

SCENE 1

Feste's lines are doubly ironical because they are in fact true (lines 15–19).

In the street near Olivia's house, Feste, the clown, has mistaken Sebastian for Cesario and is insisting that Olivia has sent for him. Sebastian is irritated by what he thinks is the clown's 'folly' and gives him money to go away.

Sir Andrew, Sir Toby and Fabian enter. They too believe that Sebastian is Cesario and Sir Andrew strikes him. In return, Sebastian gives Sir Andrew a sound beating. Feste immediately goes off to report this to Olivia. Sir Toby decides to intervene and grabs hold of Sebastian. They draw their swords and are about to fight, when Olivia enters.

Olivia, also believing that Sebastian is Cesario, asks him to go into the house. She reprimands Sir Toby for his lack of manners and tells him to get out of her sight: 'Rudesby, be gone!'(line 49). Sir Toby, Sir Andrew and Fabian exit.

When she is alone with Sebastian, Olivia apologises for her uncle's behaviour. She tells him that when he hears of the 'pranks' Sir Toby has got up to in the past, he will smile. The wretched Sir Toby had made her afraid that someone dear to her heart was in danger, she confides. Sebastian is amazed at all this. He is being wooed by a beautiful woman whom he has never seen before. Is he mad? Or is he dreaming? Whichever is the case, he happily agrees to do whatever she asks.

COMMENT   The theme of mistaken identity continues with the reappearance of Sebastian. He does not know what Feste is talking about and Feste thinks he is Cesario. The audience, however, knows why they are confused – an excellent example of comically effective dramatic irony (see Literary Terms): 'Nothing that is, is so' (lines 8–9).

The comic results of a mistaken identity are taken further by Sir Andrew's reaction to Sebastian, whom he takes to be the 'coward', Cesario.

Sir Toby is now very much out of favour with his niece and this will influence the comic sub-plot (see Literary Terms) against Malvolio – Act IV Scene 2 lines 69–73.

The scene develops the turn of events which begin to resolve the problems and confusions of the main plot. Olivia believes that Cesario does indeed love her when Sebastian agrees to be 'ruled' by her: 'Madam, I will' (line 65). Obviously they are going to get married.

GLOSSARY   **Cockney** feeble thing
worse payment blows
a good report ... purchase a good reputation, provided they pay well for it
an action of battery legal suit for assault
dear Cesario (Olivia uses Cesario's name to underline the dramatic irony)
Beshrew ... for me my curse upon him
What relish is this? i.e. What does this mean?
Lethe in classical mythology this was the river of oblivion in Hades

Y

SCENE 2

Are we able to feel any sympathy for Malvolio at this point?

Malvolio has been locked in a dark room to cure him of his 'midsummer madness'. Maria and Feste, the clown, enter and prepare one final trick on the puritanical steward. Feste dresses up as a priest, 'Sir Topas', who will interview Malvolio. Maria goes off to fetch Sir Toby. When 'Sir Topas' talks to Malvolio he uses obscure Latin phrases and pseudo-philosophical arguments. The steward is 'relieved to hear a priest's voice' and thinks he will soon be released. This does not happen: he will remain in 'darkness' for some time. 'Sir Topas' leaves Malvolio crying for help.

Sir Toby, who has been brought back by Maria, tells the clown to assume his normal voice and speak to Malvolio. The knight wants to put an end to this 'knavery' because he is out of favour with Olivia. He is worried that his niece will turn him out of the house.

Feste goes once more into the dark room, this time singing a popular song in his own voice. When Malvolio recognises him, he asks for 'a candle, and pen, ink, and paper' (line 84) so that he can send a message to Olivia. In the darkness Feste makes Malvolio believe there are two people present by alternating his own voice with that of 'Sir Topas'. Malvolio asserts that he is not insane and that he has been 'notoriously abused' (line 90). The clown goes off, singing, to fetch the writing materials.

COMMENT

As before, a disguise is used to create comedy.

The scene's dramatic function is to let the sub-plot (see Literary Terms) move towards its end. Sir Toby is keen to bring the joke to an end more out of self-interest than any concern for Malvolio.

A parson's black gown is used here which is, ironically, the colour normally associated with Malvolio, who in contrast is dressed in bright colours. This reversal provides a visual symbol of just how thoroughly his pride has been humiliated.

Feste says 'there is no darkness but ignorance' (lines 43–4) and Malvolio's ignorance has been ruthlessly exposed in the scene. He was ignorant to think that Olivia could ever love him in the first place.

GLOSSARY   **dissemble, dissembled** (1) disguise (2) be a hypocrite

good housekeeper a hospitable person

Bonos dies good day

hyperbolical vehement

puzzled lost, hopeless

any constant reasoning any test of intelligence

Nay, I am for all waters I can turn my hand to anything

propertied me treated me like a senseless object

face me out of my wits insolently insist that I'm mad

Advise you Be careful

shent rebuked

the old Vice a stock character in morality plays

SCENE 3   Sebastian sits alone in Olivia's garden reflecting on what has happened. Unexpectedly he is loved by a beautiful young countess who has given him a love token, a pearl; he can hardly believe his good fortune and wonders what has happened to Antonio. When he called at The Elephant he was told that Antonio was roving around the town looking for him. If only his trusted friend were here now, then he could perhaps give Sebastian some good advice. Although he knows that he is not deluded, the circumstances are so strange that he is prepared to believe that either he or Olivia is mad.

Soon Olivia enters accompanied by a priest. She asks Sebastian not to blame her for being in such a hurry, but she wishes him to go with her straightaway to her private chapel and marry her. The marriage will be kept secret until an appropriate time occurs for it to be made public. Sebastian agrees wholeheartedly and they exit.

COMMENT

Note that Olivia never addresses Sebastian as 'Cesario'. This would make it impossible for the audience to maintain belief in the marriage ceremony where naturally Cesario would have to be named. Shakespeare was not as concerned about these little points of realistic detail as a modern dramatist would be.

This is a romantic comedy and a happy ending, usually symbolised by a marriage, is called for. Sebastian questions the plausibility of it all, but accepts Olivia's invitation to the church without question. If we find ourselves denying that such an 'improbable fiction' (Act III Scene 4 lines 128–9) could take place, Shakespeare has anticipated our objections by incorporating this view in the dialogue. The couplets at the end (lines 132–5) reinforce the sense of artificiality and distance.

GLOSSARY

was had been

credit report

my soul disputes well with my sense my reason agrees with the evidence of my senses

deceivable deceptive

chantry part of a church, or a chapel

whiles until

our celebration keep celebrate our marriage ceremony

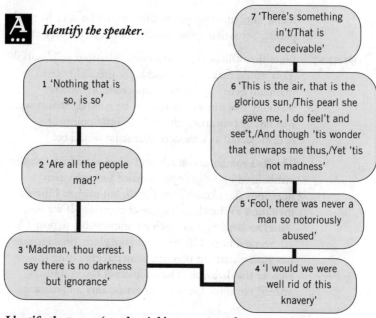

A *Identify the speaker.*

7 'There's something in't/That is deceivable'

1 'Nothing that is so, is so'

6 'This is the air, that is the glorious sun,/This pearl she gave me, I do feel't and see't,/And though 'tis wonder that enwraps me thus,/Yet 'tis not madness'

2 'Are all the people mad?'

5 'Fool, there was never a man so notoriously abused'

3 'Madman, thou errest. I say there is no darkness but ignorance'

4 'I would we were well rid of this knavery'

Identify the person 'to whom' this comment refers.

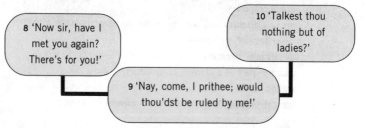

8 'Now sir, have I met you again? There's for you!'

10 'Talkest thou nothing but of ladies?'

9 'Nay, come, I prithee; would thou'dst be ruled by me!'

Check your answers on page 87.

B *Consider these issues.*

a The part disguise and mistaken identity continues to play in the act as a whole.

b How Shakespeare develops the character of Sebastian.

c The role of Feste in Scenes 1 and 2.

d How far we are able to feel sympathy for Malvolio.

e The urgency with which Olivia marries Sebastian.

ACT V

SCENE 1

The dialogue alternates between verse and prose, reflecting the moods of the main plot and sub-plot.

In the street outside Olivia's house, Feste is on his way to deliver Malvolio's letter. He is intercepted by Fabian who tries unsuccessfully to persuade the clown to let him see the letter.

The duke enters with his entourage, Cesario (Viola), Curio and some noble men. The clown entertains them with witty conversation and Duke Orsino is pleased by this – he gives Feste a gold coin and orders him to announce to Olivia that he has come to see her.

While they are waiting Antonio is brought on by some officers. Cesario tells the duke that this is the man who intervened in his duel with Sir Andrew. Orsino recognises Antonio's face, even though the last time he saw it, it was 'besmear'd/As black as Vulcan, in the smoke of war' (lines 50–1). Antonio had been the captain of a tiny pirate ship which, in spite of its size, had fought heroically against the most powerful of the duke's vessels.

Antonio protests that although he was at that time Orsino's enemy, he was never a pirate. He goes on to explain how he has come to be in Illyria, and he points at Cesario who he still believes is Sebastian. He claims he has been bewitched by the 'ingrateful boy' (line 75) who is standing at Orsino's side. I rescued him from a shipwreck, he says, and cared for him with love and devotion for three months. In return, complains Antonio, he has denied he knows me and refused to give me back my money.

Olivia enters with her attendants and Orsino immediately turns his attention to her, telling Antonio that Cesario has been his servant for the last three months and therefore Antonio's talk is 'madness'.

Olivia is annoyed. She asks Orsino what she can do for him and then accuses Cesario of failing to keep an appointment with her. Orsino becomes very angry with Olivia and his frustration makes him turn on Cesario, whom he knows Olivia loves. He threatens to kill him out of spite for Olivia. Cesario consents to follow

Orsino goes through rapid changes of emotion in the scene.

Orsino and submit to whatever fate he has in store for him, for he loves Orsino more than his life, 'More, by all mores, than e'er I shall love wife' (line 134). Olivia is horrified, and she calls for the priest who married her to Cesario (in reality to Sebastian). The priest enters and confirms that he did indeed marry them only two hours before. An enraged Orsino turns on Cesario and orders him to leave his sight forever. Cesario (Viola) tries to protest but is stopped by Olivia.

Sir Andrew enters crying out for a surgeon. He and Sir Toby have been wounded by Cesario, he claims. Sir Andrew's head has been broken and Sir Toby has a 'bloody coxcomb' (line 174). Cesario (Viola) protests that he did not hurt Sir Andrew when the knight drew his sword, but merely spoke politely to him. Drunk and bleeding, Sir Toby comes on the scene with the clown, Feste, who tells him that the surgeon cannot attend because he is drunk. Sir Toby curses the surgeon: 'I hate a drunken rogue' (line 199), he says.

Olivia soon puts a stop to all this 'havoc' by sending Sir Toby off to bed and he departs while fighting off the unwanted attentions of Sir Andrew. The clown and Fabian follow them.

Sebastian, the cause of all this confusion, now enters. He apologises to Olivia for injuring her uncle but explains that he would have had to do the same even if it had been his own brother, in order to protect himself. He notices that Olivia is looking at him strangely and concludes she is very offended, but like Orsino and Antonio, Olivia is simply amazed at the extraordinary likeness between Sebastian and Cesario. And when

Several different forms of 'recognition' occur.

Sebastian sees Cesario he too is astonished to see someone who looks so like himself – 'Do I stand there?' (line 224) – and asks him if they are related. Cesario (Viola) tells him that he looks very like a twin brother called Sebastian who drowned in a 'watery tomb' (line 232), and that Cesario's father was called 'Sebastian' also. Sebastian could be this brother's ghost.

As soon as Sebastian and Viola (Cesario) realise they had the same father, Viola reveals herself as Sebastian's lost sister. She says that she can confirm this by taking Sebastian to the sea captain who has been keeping her woman's clothes all this while, the same sea captain who helped her to disguise herself as 'Cesario' and serve the Duke Orsino as a messenger in the 'business' of his wooing Olivia.

Sebastian informs Olivia that she has been 'mistook' and would have been married to a virgin girl if she had married 'Cesario' but since she in fact married him, Sebastian, she has married a virgin youth ('a maid and man'). The duke turns to Viola and reminds her that, as 'Cesario', she had claimed many times that she would never love a woman as much as she loved him. He takes her hand and asks to see her dressed in her 'woman's weeds' (line 271). Viola replies that the captain who has her clothes is at present being kept in prison by Malvolio. Olivia calls for Malvolio to be brought before them so that the captain can be released and Feste returns carrying the steward's letter. Olivia orders the clown to read the letter out loud, but the affected voice he puts on is too distracting, so she asks Fabian to read it. The duke does not believe a true madman could have written such a letter and Olivia tells Fabian to bring Malvolio before them.

Malvolio arrives clutching the love letter which he believes Olivia had written to him. Olivia instantly

Malvolio speaks in blank verse for the first and only time in the play (lines 329–43).

recognises her servant, Maria's, handwriting. She sees that Malvolio has been made the victim of a very clever practical joke and promises him that when more is known about it, he shall be both 'plaintiff and judge' (line 353) in the case.

'Tell me, why?' (line 343) – Malvolio has not learned anything about his character.

Fabian gives an account of the plot to make a fool of Malvolio and relates why they wanted to get revenge on the steward, those 'stubborn and uncourteous parts' (line 360) which had offended them. He says that Maria wrote the letter at Sir Toby's instigation and the knight was so pleased by it that he has married her 'in recompense'.

Olivia expresses pity for the 'poor fool' (line 368) Malvolio and Feste taunts him with some of the phrases from the letter and the 'Sir Topas' episode. This is the way time brings in its revenges, he gloats. The enraged Malvolio exits, threatening his own revenge on all of them.

Duke Orsino then promises a harmonious union between Viola and himself, for when she has exchanged her male disguise for her woman's clothes, she will be 'Orsino's mistress, and his fancy's queen' (line 387).

All the characters leave except Feste, the clown, who sings a final song to end the play.

COMMENT The single scene of the final act provides a strong sense of cohesion because it is within this last scene that all the plots, mistakes and confusions have to be resolved.

The conversation in prose between Orsino and the clown establishes a light-hearted mood. Feste is carrying Malvolio's letter to Olivia which will later resolve the sub-plot (see Literary Terms) of his gulling.

The confusions caused by the various mistaken identities are brought to a climax after the introduction of Antonio. He accuses Cesario of betraying him. Then Olivia, also believing Cesario is Sebastian, accuses him of betraying their marriage vows. And Orsino accuses Cesario of alienating this love for Olivia.

Shakespeare makes the audience wait a little longer for the resolution of these mistakes by bringing on Sir Andrew and Sir Toby, bruised and bleeding from their encounter with Sebastian. They in turn accuse the disguised Viola of assaulting them. Their description of 'Cesario' as a 'very devil incardinate' (line 179) makes a humourous contrast to the civilised and gentle Viola known to the audience.

The appearance of Sebastian constitutes the resolution of all these mistakes, the recognition which the audience has been waiting for. When reading the play it is important to visualise this moment and imagine both twins dressed as men and therefore impossible for the other characters to tell apart.

The focus of this final part of the scene is on Sebastian, because Viola must gradually come to recognise her lost brother, just as Sebastian himself must come to recognise his lost sister through her disguise as 'Cesario'.

True to the conventions of romantic comedy all the main characters end up partnered off – Olivia with Sebastian, Orsino with Viola, and we learn that even Sir Toby has married Maria.

Only Malvolio is left outside this harmonious conclusion: he contributes a disturbing note of anger and resentment after he has learned the facts of his deception.

GLOSSARY

baubling ridiculously small

bottom ship

fraught from Candy freight from Crete

desperate of shame and state recklessly unconcerned about his shameful past and present behaviour

th'Egyptian thief Thyamis, in Heliodorus' *Ethiopica*, tried to kill his beloved captive, Charichea

marble-breasted tyrant a conventional image in Elizabethan love poetry

passy measures pavin passamezzo pavan, a slow and stately dance of eight bars. (Suitable for the surgeon, whose eyes are 'set at eight' – line 197)

nature to her bias drew nature followed her normal tendency

glass the natural perspective

extracting frenzy a madness that obliterated (all thoughts of Malvolio's madness)

the whirligig of Time time's spinning top

convents is suitable

fancy's love's

A Identify the speaker.

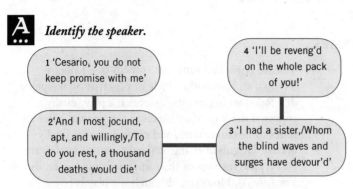

1 'Cesario, you do not keep promise with me'

2 'And I most jocund, apt, and willingly,/To do you rest, a thousand deaths would die'

3 'I had a sister,/Whom the blind waves and surges have devour'd'

4 'I'll be reveng'd on the whole pack of you!'

Identify the person 'to whom' this comment refers.

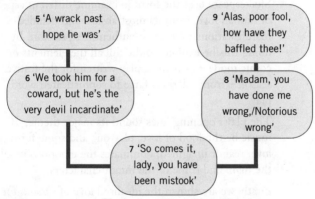

5 'A wrack past hope he was'

6 'We took him for a coward, but he's the very devil incardinate'

7 'So comes it, lady, you have been mistook'

8 'Madam, you have done me wrong,/Notorious wrong'

9 'Alas, poor fool, how have they baffled thee!'

Check your answers on page 87.

B Consider these issues.

a How Shakespeare resolves the sub-plot (see Literary Terms) and the main plot.

b What Duke Orsino says about Antonio.

c Which characters play the most important part in bringing about the various recognitions.

d The language and emotions of Orsino before and after the mutual recognition of the twins.

e The treatment of Sir Andrew by Sir Toby.

f Malvolio's response to the facts of his deception.

g The part dramatic convention plays at the very end of the scene.

PART THREE

COMMENTARY

THEMES

Twelfth Night is a romantic comedy (see Literary Terms), an Elizabethan style of play that Shakespeare developed with great success. Such a play usually concerns the love of an idealised couple who, after a series of misadventures, and confusions, are finally united. Disguised characters and a remote setting are also typical features of the romantic comedy (see also *As You Like It*). However, although the play is termed a 'comedy', its themes are essentially serious, and Shakespeare uses the form to examine different aspects of human love, from its most absurd and deluded manifestations to its most authentic expression. In doing this he exploits to the full all the elements of the comic mode – as befits a play written for the festive season – from hilarious farce to sophisticated word-play.

LOVE

The play's opening lines sound its major theme, 'If music be the food of love, play on', and some form of love, real or imagined, dominates the emotions of all the main and some of the minor characters.

Firstly we are shown the idealised love of Orsino for Olivia whom he loves at a distance and through the messages he sends with Viola (Cesario). Such a lover is not dismayed by the fact that its object cannot respond; on the contrary, Orsino sees Olivia's decision to mourn her brother's death and live like a nun as proof of her 'sweet perfections' (I.1.39). Orsino's love is self-regarding and egotistical; he sees himself as typical of all true lovers and refuses to accept rejection. He is prone to generalisations on the nature of love while unaware of how close he is to genuine feeling when he talks to Viola dressed as Cesario in Act II Scene 4.

Such deluded aspects of love are echoed in the love

Olivia feels for Cesario. But here the deception is based on physical appearance. Olivia falls rapidly in love with 'this youth's perfections' and yet fears that her 'eye' has misled her into love (I.5.302). The deluded lover is parodied in the sub-plot (see Literary Terms) through the figure of Malvolio who believes unquestioningly that his beautiful mistress loves him.

There are five unrequited lovers in the play - three in the main plot and two in the sub-plot.

Both Orsino and Malvolio are in different ways governed by the 'self-love' which Olivia accuses Malvolio of at the end of Act I Scene 5 (line 89) and the play's treatment of love seems to propose a distinction between love that is based on vanity or ambition, and love that is genuine and selfless. Viola's love for Orsino is an example of the latter. She endures with patience the 'barful strife' of her situation, wooing another woman for the man she secretly loves, and only able to express her feelings indirectly. Another example of selfless love is in the loyalty and care with which Antonio treats Sebastian.

DISGUISE

'Nothing that is so, is so' (IV.1.8–9)

Women's parts were played by boy actors in Shakespeare's day, so the original Elizabethan audience would have found a special sophistication in Viola's part: a boy dressing up as a woman who, in the play, disguises herself as a man. Viola's disguise, in fact, is central to the plot. It enables the audience to know more of the true situation when Olivia and Orsino are on stage, and it is the cause of many of the dramatic complications and confusions which make up the story.

Many forms of disguise feature in the play. Emotions and intentions are disguised behind an outer appearance, a pretence, or an attitude. Olivia's pretence at mourning is quickly discarded when she meets Cesario. Orsino's love for Olivia can be seen as an elaborate pretence when it gives way to murderous anger in Act V, before he rapidly transfers his affections to Viola. Feste adopts a disguise to torment Malvolio in Act IV. Sir Toby Belch disguises his real motives behind his show of friendship for Sir Andrew Aguecheek. And even Malvolio's yellow stockings and cross garters are a kind of masquerade.

The dramatic convention of disguise produces ambiguities of meaning and emotion throughout the play.

The play abounds in references to these different forms of disguise, to the gap between what appears to be true and what really is. Viola calls disguise 'a wickedness/ Wherein the pregnant enemy does much' (II.2.26–7) when she realises that Olivia has fallen in love with her persona as Cesario. In the play's moral scheme, disguise or self-deception create frustration and confusion. Antonio, for example, in Act III Scene 4, regrets the 'devotion' which Sebastian's handsome features had inspired in him (lines 374–8). Ironically, though, he is mistaken; yet his generalisations on the nature of virtue are relevant to the play as a whole.

Disguised characters were a stock convention of comedy, but Shakespeare uses the device to give it wider significance. The play makes us consider what our beliefs about ourselves and others are based upon. The action of the play brings the true natures of Olivia, Orsino and Malvolio to the surface, and only Malvolio at the end seems unable to recognise himself, blinded as he is by pride and self-righteousness.

THE FESTIVE SPIRIT

The importance of pleasure, tolerance and generosity are emphasised in *Twelfth Night*, as befits a play written to be performed during the Christmas season. The 'Twelfth Night' festivities, held on 6 January, were celebrated by Queen Elizabeth and her court with a great banquet followed by an entertainment. If the play was indeed written for such an occasion, then we have no difficulty accounting for its mixture of impossible

romance, slapstick comedy and satire. These ingredients
would have been the order of the day in a festival which
descended from the ancient Roman 'Saturnalia' and the
medieval 'Feast of Fools'. The characters can be divided
between those who have a straightforward commitment
to pleasure and the 'good life', and those who don't.
The former group are led by Sir Toby, and his opening
lines provide a clear statement of his philosophy: he
deplores his young niece's vow to spend seven years in
mourning – 'I am sure care's an enemy to life' (I.3.2–3).
The melancholic atmosphere in Olivia's house is in
opposition to the carefree values of Sir Toby and when
Malvolio is sent to stop the carousing in Act II Scene 3
the conflict between pleasure and its denial is brought
to a head. 'Dost thou think because thou art virtuous
there shall be no more cakes and ale?' (II.3.114–5) – Sir
Toby's blunt question to Malvolio sums up the anti-
puritan values which are shared by Feste, Sir Andrew
and Maria. It is as much for this puritanism, as his
conceit and arrogance, that Malvolio will be punished
by the revellers.

The play celebrates
love and pleasure
in the present, for
human life is
short.

A carpe diem (see Literary Terms) theme runs through
the play. This is the invitation to enjoy youth and life
quickly, in the present, for it will soon pass. Feste's
song (Act II Scene 3) expresses his plea: 'What is love?
'Tis not hereafter,/Present mirth hath present
laughter:/What's to come is still unsure' (lines 47–50).
Both Olivia and Orsino are failing to 'seize the day' in
their respective attitudes of nun and passive lover. In his
role as commentator on the 'folly' of his superiors, Feste
alludes to the fact that Olivia's sorrow will quickly pass:
'As there is no true cuckold but calamity, so beauty's a
flower' (I.5.49–50). He is suggesting that Olivia's
mourning is foolish and she that should be giving her
young life to love.

Sebastian, Antonio, Viola, and even finally Olivia,

embody the values of generosity which the play evokes. Sebastian, in Act III Scene 3, is concerned to reward Antonio for his devotion – 'uncurrent pay' (mere thanks) is not enough, he fears. And Antonio himself has displayed selfless giving in his loyalty to Sebastian, not least through providing him with money and protection in a strange land. When Viola first meets Olivia she accuses her of keeping the gifts of beauty which nature has given her to herself: 'Lady, you are the cruell'st she alive/If you will lead these graces to the grave/And leave the world no copy' (I.5.245–6). Viola has a frank, loving nature. Her eloquent call to love in the scene arouses Olivia's feelings, even though ironically they are directed at 'Cesario'. Olivia 'speaks for the virtues of generous loving' when she criticises Malvolio for his lack of a 'free disposition' (I.5.91) – his lack of magnanimity, and when, in Act III Scene 1, she tells Viola that 'Love sought is good, but given unsought is better' (line 158).

STRUCTURE

Although *Twelfth Night* can be divided into a main plot and a number of sub-plots (see Literary Terms) a useful way to approach its structure is to think first of the way different groups of characters are interwoven to make up a single texture. Firstly, there are the aristocratic characters, Duke Orsino and the Countess Olivia, whose situation is given in the opening scene. Then there are the shipwrecked twins, Viola and Sebastian, and their helpers, a sea captain and Antonio. The fate of these characters is the business of the main plot. A third group is made up of the revellers, Sir Toby Belch, Sir Andrew Aguecheek, Maria, Fabian and Feste, the clown. Their actions constitute the sub-plots. Between these groups moves the connecting figure of Feste, who clowns for Olivia and sings for Orsino, and who is part of the plan to gull Malvolio. Outside all of this, Olivia's

Have a clear idea of how the characters are grouped before reading the text. This will make the story easier to understand.

egotistical steward stands in isolation.

Shakespeare took the love story of *Twelfth Night* from a short story called *The Historie of Apolonius and Silla* which in turn derives from an Italian play, *Gl'Ingannati* (1531). In *Twelfth Night* we find a number of conventions (disguise, gender confusion, twins – see Literary Terms) which are common to previous dramas being given fresh subtleties. For example, in the duel scene Viola's fear contains an element of realism which Shakespeare has introduced to an originally stock situation (see Literary Terms) – as a woman she will have no knowledge of fighting.

The standard Elizabethan five-act form allows Shakespeare to develop, scene by scene, alternating aspects of each of the plots. Acts I and II are an exposition in which all the basic situations are set up. Act III moves towards a climax, the appearance of Malvolio in yellow stockings and cross garters. The three short scenes of Act IV prepare the resolution of all the complications that will take place in the long single scene of Act V. Within this framework Shakespeare controls the audience's response and expectations with considerable skill. By the end of Act I four situations have been given which provide the impetus for the rest of the play:

- Orsino's unrequited love for Olivia
- Sir Toby's unruly behaviour in Olivia's house and his self-interested friendship with the rich Sir Andrew Aguecheek
- Viola's disguised love for Orsino
- Olivia's love for Cesario

The plot of a comedy takes the main characters from failure to success.

All these situations are potentially disastrous (imagine the same predicaments treated in the tragic mode), yet *Twelfth Night* is a comedy and the audience expects a happy ending. Shakespeare signals the possibility of such an ending by introducing Sebastian at the start of Act II: we know he is going to play an important part in the solution to the 'problem' because he goes off to Orsino's court. To emphasise the 'problem', Shakespeare allows Viola an opportunity to articulate it in her soliloquy (see Literary Terms) at the end of Act II Scene 2 (lines 16–40); like her, the audience is made to expect 'time' (i.e. the action of the play) to unravel the 'knot'.

The chief sub-plot, the gulling of Malvolio, provides a parallel and comic contrast to the more serious plot featuring the aristocratic figures of Orsino and Olivia, Viola and Sebastian. It gets properly underway in Act II Scene 3, after Malvolio interrupts the drinking party. Shakespeare has carefully prepared the audience's response to this by depicting Malvolio in previous scenes as an increasingly unsympathetic figure, both through his own words and actions, and through the words of other characters (e.g. Act I Scene 5 and Act II Scene 2). Another sub-plot, also featuring Sir Toby and his friends, is interlocked with the gulling of Malvolio: Sir Andrew Aguecheek's foolish belief that he could marry Olivia which is taken up in Act III. Both sub-plots feature an absurd letter and an absurd suitor for Olivia.

The play has a logical structure developing from what we already know, raising expectations and providing surprising incidents.

In the structure of *Twelfth Night* the actions that anticipate future events and raise audience expectations can be summarised as follows:

- Viola's assumption of a disguise (Act I Scene 2)
- Sir Toby persuades Sir Andrew to stay and woo Olivia (Act I Scene 3)
- The appearance of Sebastian (Act II Scene 1)
- Viola's soliloquy (Act II Scene 2)
- Malvolio's behaviour (Act I Scene 5 and Act II Scene 2)

- When Sir Toby and Sir Andrew meet 'Cesario' (Act III Scene 1)
- When Antonio gives Sebastian money (Act III Scene 3)
- When Antonio calls Cesario (Viola) 'Sebastian' (Act III Scene 4)

CHARACTERS

ORSINO

Melancholic

In love with love

Eloquent and poetic

Inconsistent

Passive

Repressed

Duke Orsino's opening speech in Act I tells us something about his character and mood; he is in love, but this does not bring him happiness, rather a profound melancholy. His speech turns to images of disease and death – 'excess ... surfeiting ... sicken ... die ... dying' – and it is clear that Orsino is not an active lover focused on his beloved. He is preoccupied with the sensation of love itself, feeding his emotions with music and elaborate poetic imagery. Orsino has probably seen Olivia only once, and her image has inspired in him a kind of romantic indulgence, a belief that if she does not love him in return, he will die. From this passive, self-regarding emotion comes his employment of Cesario (Viola) as a messenger who will do his wooing for him.

Orsino is an inconsistent character as Feste points out in Act II Scene 4, with a mind of 'opal'. He begs for music to reflect his mood, then quickly becomes bored. This changeable nature, however, makes believable his sudden transference of affection from Olivia to Viola at the end of the play. Perhaps his sudden outburst of anger in the final scene indicates repressed aspects of his character.

However, if Viola is to fall in love with Orsino, then his character must justify this to the audience. He is described by Olivia in Act I Scene 5 as 'virtuous ... noble ...', a wealthy, well-educated, courteous and handsome man. These are the qualities that make Viola fall in love with him.

VIOLA

Practical
Resourceful
Accomplished
Trusting
Intelligent
Loyal
Honest
Depth of feeling

Viola stands between the two extremes of emotion represented by Orsino and Olivia and as such she embodies a kind of norm of behaviour in the heady atmosphere of Illyria.

From our first encounter with her in Act I we learn that she is a practical person who makes the best of her situation as a shipwrecked orphan, and a woman in a strange land. Her decision to disguise herself as a eunuch denotes both courage and resourcefulness. She is trusting enough to take the sea captain's help and resolves to use her accomplishments to gain employment in Orsino's court.

Viola reveals her intelligence, wit (see Literary Terms) and charm throughout the play, qualities that enable her to gain Orsino's special confidence and that cause Olivia to fall in love with her at first sight. Her conversations with Orsino and Olivia show that she is an honest straightforward character in spite of the deception she is forced to enact for her own survival. She loyally continues to try to win Olivia's love for Orsino, even though she loves him herself. And she treats Olivia with dignity when the countess has confessed her love for her (as Cesario). Her capacity for deep feeling is clear from the story she tells Orsino in Act II Scene 4: 'My father had a daughter lov'd a man …' (lines 108–16).

OLIVIA

We learn a good deal about Olivia before she actually appears on the stage in the last scene of Act I. Her beauty is the cause of Orsino's poetic love in the first scene; in Scene 2 the captain tells Viola about the 'virtuous maid' who had been orphaned and lost a brother; the third scene is set in her house; she is the subject of the conversation between Orsino and Cesario in Scene 4. She is therefore a character much anticipated by the audience by the time she finally appears.

Virtuous
Melancholic
Self-deceived
Intelligent
Impetuous
Compassionate

On the face of it, Olivia's melancholy, her extravagant vow to mourn her brother for seven years, counter-balances the excessive romantic melancholy of Orsino. She is thus capable of self-deception, as the play subsequently demonstrates.

But Olivia has other, more attractive qualities. She is seen as intelligent and adaptable in her dealings with other members of her household – she soon allows Feste to win her over with his clowning, and her characterisation of Malvolio is cogent (Act I Scene 5). And her response to Malvolio's humiliation reveals a compassionate nature.

The quality that most characterises Olivia, however, is her capacity for impetuous feeling. She pursues Cesario relentlessly, with little concern for the decorum demanded by her own status as a countess and 'his' as a servant. Although she is able to rationalise Orsino's attractive qualities, she has no difficulty rejecting him as a lover. The comic irony of her situation lies partly in this irrational pursuit of Cesario.

Like Orsino, her feelings at the end are quickly transferred from one object of love to another.

SIR TOBY BELCH

Carefree
Irresponsible
Witty
Manipulative
Self-interested

Olivia's uncle is a large, earthy and jolly knight who is devoted to pleasures of the flesh, as his name suggests and as his behaviour throughout the play indicates. He is also a keen-witted person, even when he is drunk, and his intelligence contrasts sharply with his dupe, Sir Andrew Aguecheek.

In his relationship with Sir Andrew, Sir Toby displays a manipulative side to his character. He fools the gullible knight into believing that he could marry Olivia so that he will remain in her house and continue to finance Sir Toby's drinking habit. He loves a practical joke, especially when it is ingenious, and for her ability to think up such a clever trick as the gulling of Malvolio, he marries Maria.

In spite of his carefree and irresponsible nature, there is something of the bully in Sir Toby. He makes fun of Sir Andrew and Malvolio only as far as his self-interest allows: when there is a real possibility that Olivia will throw him out of the house, he loses interest in the two gulls.

MALVOLIO

Puritanical
Self-important
Humourless
Vain
Self-deluded

Malvolio is Olivia's steward and an important member of her household. But he is not as important as he would like to be. He is socially inferior to Sir Toby and deeply resents the irresponsible knight's riotous behaviour.

Malvolio is always serious and he has absolutely no sense of humour. He believes in dignity, good manners and order. He is always dressed in black.

In the play Malvolio is revealed as a hypocrite and an egotist. Beneath the puritanical exterior resides a vain, intolerant, ambitious personality whose conceit makes him an easy target for the practical jokers.

At the end of the play Malvolio is excluded from the general happiness and good fortune of the other main characters. He is incapable of self-knowledge.

MINOR CHARACTERS

Sir Andrew Auguecheek	A tall, thin and very stupid knight. He is staying in Olivia's house at the invitation of Sir Toby Belch.He is rich, and Sir Toby encourages him to continue wooing the inaccessible countess so that he will finance their regular drinking sessions.
Maria	Olivia's waiting-gentlewoman. She is sharp-witted, practical and inventive; she devises and manages the trick that is played on Malvolio. She eventually marries Sir Toby.

Feste

A clown employed by the Countess Olivia. His role in the play is to provide music and witty comment. His foolery is everywhere, since he moves freely between the households of both Olivia and Orsino. This and his critical attitude towards the other characters makes him appear a rather detached characeter. He is very good at his job (as Viola recognises in III.1.60) and is paid for his wit on several occasions in the course of the play.

Apart from singing and providing verbal repartee, he is enrolled to participate in slapstick comedy when he dresses as 'Sir Topas'. Feste represents the festive spirit of the play, but there is also something touchy and cynical about him.

Sebastian

Viola's twin brother who she becomes separated from after the shipwreck. Like his sister, he is helped by a sea captain (Antonio) to make his way to Illyria. He is mistaken for Cesario and marries Olivia.

A handsome, modest and courageous man, Sebastian is rather more emotional than his sister (Viola) and grieves deeply when he thinks she has drowned in the shipwreck. He appreciated Antonio's loyalty but does not want to cause him any misfortune.

As the masculine counterpart to Viola (Cesario) he becomes Olivia's 'natural' husband.

Antonio

A sea captain who rescues and befriends Sebastian. He risks his life to follow Sebastian and is arrested by Orsino's officers.

Fabian

A servant of Olivia's. He participates in the gulling of Malvolio and later assists Sir Toby in the trick that is played on Sir Andrew and Cesario.

Valentine and Curio

Two gentlemen attending on the Duke Orsino.

A sea captain

The captain of the wrecked ship who helps Viola with her disguise. He appears only once in the play.

In Shakespeare's plays the language is of primary importance. The Elizabethan actors were expected to deliver their lines with an emphasis on the expressive power of the words. The representation of character through, for example, gesture or facial expression was secondary to this. Therefore, in a way, the flow of language is where the action is; like a musical score it forms a complex pattern of sound and meaning.

Shakespeare basically uses three styles of writing in his dialogue; poetic verse, blank verse (see Literary Terms) and prose. We will look at examples of all three and then you should find others as you read and study the play.

Poetic verse

'Enough, no more;/'Tis not so sweet now as it was before./O spirit of love, how quick and fresh art thou,/That notwithstanding thy capacity/Receiveth as the sea, nought enters there,/Of what validity and pitch soe'er,/But falls into abatement and low price,/Even in a minute! So full of shapes is fancy,/That it alone is high fantastical'. (I.1.7–15)

Here Orsino is revealing his inner emotional state in language that is both 'poetic' and psychologically realistic. The rhyming words, e.g. 'more … before' indicate his rather literary, formal expression of love. Note also the alliterations (see Literary Terms) in 'capacity … receiveth … sea'. The diction (see Literary Terms) is mostly made up of abstract words, 'spirit of love … capacity … validity … pitch' and the simile (see Literary Terms) of the vast sea implies the vague and generalising aspect of his temperament (see Feste's comment on Orsino i.e. II.4.75–9).

Blank verse

Blank verse is different to poetic verse in Shakespeare in that it does not rhyme, except sometimes in the last two lines of a speech where an emphasis may be required. It has the same rhythm or metre of five iambs (see Literary Terms) and is close to the stresses of spoken

English. It is very flexible and long sentences can be built up into verse paragraphs (see Literary Terms).

'Well, grant it then,/And tell me, in the modesty of honour,/Why you have given me such clear lights of favour,/Bade me come smiling and cross-garter'd to you,/To put on yellow stockings, and to frown/Upon Sir Toby, and the lighter people' (V.1.333–8).

This is the only time in the play that Malvolio speaks in blank verse. Note the way the lines accommodate the argumentative tone and the feel of normal conversational English in the accumulated clauses. The metaphor (see Literary Terms), 'clear lights', recalls Malvolio's exclamation 'Daylight and champaign discovers not more!' (II.5.160), after he read the forged letter.

Prose

Prose is most often given to minor or comic characters in the play. Sometimes it is used to develop the plot or provide important information about a character or an event; for example, when Olivia characterises Malvolio in Act I Scene 5, she speaks in prose which is memorable for its eloquent perception of his character. About half of the dialogue of *Twelfth Night* is in prose.

'She did show favour to the youth in your sight only to exasperate you, to awake your dormouse valour, to put fire in your heart, and brimstone in your liver. You should then have accosted her, and with some excellent jests, fire-new from the mint, you should have banged the youth into dumbness' (III.2.16–22).

Fabian's speech to Sir Andrew has a rhetorical verve and humour which is irresistible. 'Brimstone in your liver' parallels 'fire in your heart' in a way that shows Shakespeare's genius for the unusual and vivid image. Although the tone is more informal and straightforward than verse, the language still contains a metaphorical (see Literary Terms) brilliance.

PART FOUR

STUDY SKILLS

HOW TO USE QUOTATIONS

One of the secrets of success in writing essays is the way you use quotations. There are five basic principles:

- Put inverted commas at the beginning and end of the quotation
- Write the quotation exactly as it appears in the original
- Do not use a quotation that repeats what you have just written
- Use the quotation so that it fits into your sentence
- Keep the quotation as short as possible

Quotations should be used to develop the line of thought in your essays.

Your comment should not duplicate what is in your quotations. For example:

Viola (in Act II, Scene 2 of *Twelfth Night*) tells us that she thinks disguises are wicked, 'Disguise, I see thou art a wickedness'.

Far more effective is to write:

Viola describes disguise as 'a wickedness'.

Always lay out the lines as they appear in the text. For example:

Viola answers Orsino's question with a riddle: 'I am all the daughters of my father's house, /And all the brothers too: and yet I know not'.

or:

'I am all the daughters of my father's house
And all the brothers too: and yet I know not'.

However, the most sophisticated way of using the writer's words is to embed them into your sentence:

It is really Malvolio's 'self-love' which makes him easy to trick.

When you use quotations in this way, you are demonstrating the ability to use text as evidence to support your ideas - not simply including words from the original to prove you have read it.

Everyone writes differently. Work through the suggestions given here and adapt the advice to suit your own style and interests. This will improve your essay-writing skills and allow your personal voice to emerge.

The following points indicate in ascending order the skills of essay writing:

- Picking out one or two facts about the story and adding the odd detail
- Writing about the text by retelling the story
- Retelling the story and adding a quotation here and there
- Organising an answer which explains what is happening in the text and giving quotations to support what you write

....

- Writing in such a way as to show that you have thought about the intentions of the writer of the text and that you understand the techniques used
- Writing at some length, giving your viewpoint on the text and commenting by picking out details to support your views
- Looking at the text as a work of art, demonstrating clear critical judgement and explaining to the reader of your essay how the enjoyment of the text is assisted by literary devices, linguistic effects and psychological insights; showing how the text relates to the time when it was written

The dotted line above represents the division between lower and higher level grades. Higher-level performance begins when you start to consider your response as a reader of the text. The highest level is reached when you offer an enthusiastic personal response and show how this piece of literature is a product of its time.

Coursework Set aside an hour or so at the start of your work to plan
essay what you have to do.

- List all the points you feel are needed to cover the task. Collect page references of information and quotations that will support what you have to say. A helpful tool is the highlighter pen: this saves painstaking copying and enables you to target precisely what you want to use.
- Focus on what you consider to be the main points of the essay. Try to sum up your argument in a single sentence, which could be the closing sentence of your essay. Depending on the essay title, it could be a statement about a character: Viola is a witty, charming and loyal character because she wins Orsino's trust within only three days; an opinion about setting: Shakespeare set *Twelfth Night* in a far away place to emphasise the mood of romance and unreality; or a judgement on a theme: I think that the main theme of *Twelfth Night* is love, because most of the characters in the play experience this emotion.
- Make a short essay plan. Use the first paragraph to introduce the argument you wish to make. In the following paragraphs develop this argument with details, examples and other possible points of view. Sum up your argument in the last paragraph. Check you have answered the question.
- Write the essay, remembering all the time the central point you are making.
- On completion, go back over what you have written to eliminate careless errors and improve expression. Read it aloud to yourself, or, if you are feeling more confident, to a relative or friend.

If you can, try to type your essay using a word processor. This will allow you to correct and improve your writing without spoiling its appearance.

Examination   The essay written in an examination often carries more
essay   marks than the coursework essay even though it is
written under considerable time pressure.

In the revision period build up notes on various aspects
of the text you are using. Fortunately, in acquiring this
set of York Notes on *Twelfth Night,* you have made a
prudent beginning! York Notes are set out to give you
vital information and help you to construct your
personal overview of the text.

Make notes with appropriate quotations about the key
issues of the set text. Go into the examination knowing
your text and having a clear set of opinions about it.

In most English Literature examinations you can take
in copies of your set books. This in an enormous
advantage although it may lull you into a false sense of
security. Beware! There is simply not enough time in an
examination to read the book from scratch.

In the   • Read the question paper carefully and remind
examination   yourself what you have to do.
- Look at the questions on your set texts to select the
  one that most interests you and mentally work out
  the points you wish to stress.
- Remind yourself of the time available and how you
  are going to use it.
- Briefly map out a short plan in note form that will
  keep your writing on track and illustrate the key
  argument you want to make.
- Then set about writing it.
- When you have finished, check through to eliminate
  errors.

To summarise,   • **Know the text**
these are keys   • **Have a clear understanding of and opinions on the storyline,**
to success   **characters, setting, themes and writer's concerns**
- **Select the right material**
- **Plan and write a clear response, continually bearing the question
  in mind**

SAMPLE ESSAY PLAN

A typical essay question on *Twelfth Night* is followed by a sample essay plan in note form. This does not present the only answer to the question, merely one answer. Do not be afraid to include your own ideas and leave out some of the ones in this sample! Remember that quotations are essential to prove and illustrate the points you make.

Describe the different forms of disguise and deception that feature in *Twelfth Night*.

Introduction
This should clearly outline how you are going to deal with the question, briefly informing the reader how you will interpret the key terms, i.e. 'disguise' and 'deception':

- Viola's disguise as Cesario
- How disguise or deception contribute to the comedy
- How some characters are deceived about their true natures

Viola's disguise as Cesario
- Enables her to work for Orsino as a messenger
- Causes Olivia to fall in love with her
- Prevents Viola from expressing her love for Orsino
- Contributes to the dramatic ironies
- Causes the complications of mistaken identity

Disguise or deception contributes to most of the comedy
- The gulling of Malvolio
- Sir Andrew is encouraged to believe he has a chance with Olivia
- Sir Andrew and Cesario are tricked into a duel
- Feste dresses up as 'Sir Topas'
- Sir Andrew mistakes Sebastian for Cesario

Some characters are deceived about their true natures
- Olivia adopts the pretence of mourning
- Orsino deludes himself that he loves Olivia
- The puritanical Malvolio is tricked into the role of Olivia's suitor and becomes a smiling 'courtier'

Conclusions   This will draw all the material you have used in the main body of the essay together, but should not just reiterate everything you have written. If possible try to add an extra idea to give the reader something to think about, e.g. word-play is also a form of disguise and the numerous puns (see Literary Terms) in the play reflect this theme on a linguistic level (see the conversation between Viola and Feste in Act III Scene 1).

FURTHER QUESTIONS

Make a plan as shown above and attempt these questions.

1 Describe the kind of love which is experienced by Orsino.
2 In what ways might we feel pity for Malvolio at the end of the play?
3 Show how Feste is connected to both the romantic and the comic plots?
4 Describe Viola's character as it is shown throughout the play

PART FIVE

CULTURAL CONNECTIONS

BROADER PERSPECTIVES

Portraiture   Tudor and Stuart paintings at the National Portrait Gallery, London, will give you some idea of the Elizabethan love of display – beautiful clothes, richly ornamented, of which the puritans so much disapproved.

Fiction   Jane Austen's *Pride and Prejudice* (Penguin, 1996 – first published 1813) is a romantic comedy from another era which is worth comparing to *Twelfth Night*. There are problems to be overcome and lovers become involved with the wrong people, e.g. Lizzie falls for the unsuitable Wickham, while Darcy, like Orsino, is blinded by pride and Lizzie by prejudice. Eventually the romantic love plot is resolved when they marry.

Film   The film, *When Harry met Sally* (1989) is a modern romantic comedy which plays on the genre's (see Literary Terms) tendency to prolong the making of the right match: the audience knows from the start that the couple will finally get together.

Try to see Trevor Nunn's version of *Twelfth Night* (1997) and compare how the film and original versions differ. Why do you think this is so?

Elizabethan romantic comedy   Other texts by Shakespeare which you should familiarise yourself with are the comedies *As You Like It* and *Much Ado About Nothing*, and, from the same period, *A Comedy of Errors*. It would also be helpful to compare *Twelfth Night* with the tragedy, *Hamlet*.

A useful, clearly written book on the subject is G.B. Harrison's *Introducing Shakespeare* (Penguin, 1966).

Shakespeare's period   *The Terrible Tudors* by Terry Deary and Neil Tongue (Scholastic Publications, 1993) provides an entertaining, informative and accessible history book on the period.

John Dover Wilson has compiled an anthology of
writings, *Life in Shakespeare's England* (Macmillan,
1913), from the Elizabethan era covering a wide range
of relevant topics. This book is probably now only
available in libraries.

alliteration a sequence of repeated sounds in a stretch of language

blank verse unrhymed iambic pentameter a line of five iambs

carpe diem (latin for 'seize the day') this denotes a theme or subject common in all literature: the plea or invitation to enjoy youth and life quickly, before the onset of dull maturity or death. This is often combined with an offer of love

Commedia dell'arte a form of drama in sixteenth-century Italy in which travelling companies of actors improvised comic plays around standard plots using stock characters

conventions all forms of literature are best understood or enjoyed when the reader or audience is aware of certain common features of the particular kind of literature in question: these common features are the 'conventions' of that form

diction the choice of words in a work of literature

dramatic irony this occurs when the development of the plot allows the audience to possess more information about what is happening than some of the characters themselves have

genre the term for a kind or type of literature. The major genres of literature are poetry, drama and the novel (prose). These can be subdivided into further genres, such as lyric, narrative verse, comedy, tragedy, short story, autobiography, biography and so on

hyperbole a figure of speech reliant on exaggeration

iamb the commonest metrical foot in English verse, a weak stress followed by a strong stress, ti-tum

iambic pentameter a line of five iambic feet. The most common metrical pattern found in English verse

metaphor a metaphor is when two different things or ideas are fused together: one thing is described as being another thing e.g. 'when the rich golden shaft/Hath kill'd the flock of all affections' (I.1.35–6)

metre this is the pattern of stressed and unstressed syllables in a line of verse

oxymoron a figure of speech in which contrasting terms are brought together: 'The Fortunate Unhappy' (II.5.159)

pathos moments in works of art which envoke strong feelins of pity and sorrow are said to have this quality

poetic verse a style of speech in Shakespeare's plays using rhyming couplets and a strong rhythmic pulse to the line

prose any language that is not patterned by the regularity of some kind of metre

pun a play on words: two widely different meanings are drawn out of a single word, usually for comic purposes

rhyming couplet a pair of rhymed lines, of any metre e.g. 'O time, thou must untangle this, not I,/It is too hard a knot for me t'untie' (II.2.139–40)

romantic comedy an Elizabethan style of comedy concerning love, difficulties often involving mistaken identities, an escape from the real world into a quasi magical setting, and a happy ending (see also *As You Like It*)

simile a figure of speech in which one thing is said to be like another, always containing the word 'like' or 'as'

soliloquy a dramatic convention which allows a character in a play to speak directly to the audience – as if thinking aloud about motives, feelings and decisions

stock characters/situations all genres make use of recurrent elements of plot, characterisation and situations which may become a defining aspect of that genre, part of its conventions. See Commedia dell'arte

sub-plot a subsidiary action running

y

parallel with the main plot of a play or novel

verse paragraph division of blank verse into large, irregular units

wit originally meaning 'sense', 'understanding' or 'intelligence', the word came to refer to the kind of poetic intelligence which combines or contrastsideas and expressions in an unexpected and intellectually pleasing way.

TEST ANSWERS

TEST YOURSELF (Act I)

A
1 Orsino *(Scene 1)*
2 Valentine *(Scene 1)*
3 Captain *(Scene 2)*
4 Viola *(Scene 2)*
5 Sir Toby Belch *(Scene 3)*
6 Sir Andrew Aguecheek *(Scene 3)*
7 Malvolio *(Scene 5)*
8 Orsino *(Scene 5)*

TEST YOURSELF (Act II)

A
1 Sebastian *(Scene 1)*
2 Viola *(Scene 2)*
3 Sir Toby Belch *(Scene 3)*
4 Maria *(Scene 3)*
5 Sir Andrew Aguecheek *(Scene 3)*
6 Malvolio *(Scene 3)*
7 Malvolio *(Scene 3)*
8 Orsino *(Scene 4)*

TEST YOURSELF (Act III)

A
1 Feste *(Scene 1)*
2 Viola *(Scene 1)*
3 Maria *(Scene 2)*
4 Antonio *(Scene 3)*
5 Malvolio *(Scene 4)*

6 Sir Andrew Aguecheek *(Scene 4)*
7 Cesario *(Scene 4)*
8 Sebastian (Cesario) *(Scene 4)*

TEST YOURSELF (Act IV)

A
1 Feste *(Scene 1)*
2 Sebastian *(Scene 1)*
3 Feste ('Sir Topas') *(Scene 2)*
4 Sir Toby Belch *(Scene 2)*
5 Malvolio *(Scene 2)*
6 Sebastian *(Scene 3)*
7 Sebastian *(Scene 3)*
8 Sebastian *(Scene 1)*
9 Sebastian *(Scene 1)*
10 Malvolio *(Scene 2)*

TEST YOURSELF (Act V)

A
1 Olivia *(Scene 1)*
2 Cesario *(Scene 1)*
3 Sebastian *(Scene 1)*
4 Malvolio *(Scene 1)*
5 Sebastian *(Scene 1)*
6 Cesario *(Scene 1)*
7 Olivia *(Scene 1)*
8 Olivia *(Scene 1)*
9 Malvolio *(Scene 1)*

NOTES

GCSE and equivalent levels (£3.50 each)

Harold Brighouse
Hobson's Choice

Charles Dickens
Great Expectations

Charles Dickens
Hard Times

George Eliot
Silas Marner

William Golding
Lord of the Flies

Thomas Hardy
The Mayor of Casterbridge

Susan Hill
I'm the King of the Castle

Barry Hines
A Kestrel for a Knave

Harper Lee
To Kill a Mockingbird

Arthur Miller
A View from the Bridge

Arthur Miller
The Crucible

George Orwell
Animal Farm

J.B. Priestley
An Inspector Calls

J.D. Salinger
The Catcher in the Rye

William Shakespeare
Macbeth

William Shakespeare
The Merchant of Venice

William Shakespeare
Romeo and Juliet

William Shakespeare
Twelfth Night

George Bernard Shaw
Pygmalion

John Steinbeck
Of Mice and Men

Mildred D. Taylor
Roll of Thunder, Hear My Cry

James Watson
Talking in Whispers

A Choice of Poets

Nineteenth Century Short Stories

Poetry of the First World War

Advanced level (£3.99 each)

Margaret Atwood
The Handmaid's Tale

Jane Austen
Emma

Jane Austen
Pride and Prejudice

William Blake
Poems/Songs of Innocence and Songs of Experience

Emily Brontë
Wuthering Heights

Geoffrey Chaucer
Wife of Bath's Prologue and Tale

Joseph Conrad
Heart of Darkness

Charles Dickens
Great Expectations

F. Scott Fitzgerald
The Great Gatsby

Thomas Hardy
Tess of the D'Urbervilles

Seamus Heaney
Selected Poems

James Joyce
Dubliners

William Shakespeare
Antony and Cleopatra

William Shakespeare
Hamlet

William Shakespeare
King Lear

William Shakespeare
Macbeth

William Shakespeare
Othello

Mary Shelley
Frankenstein

Alice Walker
The Color Purple

John Webster
The Duchess of Malfi

FUTURE TITLES IN THE YORK NOTES SERIES

Chinua Achebe
Things Fall Apart

Edward Albee
Who's Afraid of Virginia Woolf?

Jane Austen
Mansfield Park

Jane Austen
Northanger Abbey

Jane Austen
Persuasion

Jane Austen
Sense and Sensibility

Samuel Beckett
Waiting for Godot

John Betjeman
Selected Poems

Robert Bolt
A Man for All Seasons

Charlotte Brontë
Jane Eyre

Robert Burns
Selected Poems

Lord Byron
Selected Poems

Geoffrey Chaucer
The Franklin's Tale

Geoffrey Chaucer
The Knight's Tale

Geoffrey Chaucer
The Merchant's Tale

Geoffrey Chaucer
The Miller's Tale

Geoffrey Chaucer
The Nun's Priest's Tale

Geoffrey Chaucer
The Pardoner's Tale

Geoffrey Chaucer
Prologue to the Canterbury Tales

Samuel Taylor Coleridge
Selected Poems

Daniel Defoe
Moll Flanders

Daniel Defoe
Robinson Crusoe

Shelagh Delaney
A Taste of Honey

Charles Dickens
Bleak House

Charles Dickens
David Copperfield

Charles Dickens
Oliver Twist

Emily Dickinson
Selected Poems

John Donne
Selected Poems

Douglas Dunn
Selected Poems

George Eliot
Middlemarch

George Eliot
The Mill on the Floss

T.S. Eliot
The Waste Land

T.S. Eliot
Selected Poems

Henry Fielding
Joseph Andrews

E.M. Forster
Howards End

E.M. Forster
A Passage to India

John Fowles
The French Lieutenant's Woman

Elizabeth Gaskell
North and South

Oliver Goldsmith
She Stoops to Conquer

Graham Greene
Brighton Rock

Graham Greene
The Heart of the Matter

Graham Greene
The Power and the Glory

Thomas Hardy
Far from the Madding Crowd

Thomas Hardy
Jude the Obscure

Thomas Hardy
The Return of the Native

Thomas Hardy
Selected Poems

L.P. Hartley
The Go-Between

Nathaniel Hawthorne
The Scarlet Letter

Ernest Hemingway
A Farewell to Arms

Ernest Hemingway
The Old Man and the Sea

Homer
The Iliad

Homer
The Odyssey

Gerard Manley Hopkins
Selected Poems

Ted Hughes
Selected Poems

Aldous Huxley
Brave New World

Henry James
Portrait of a Lady

Ben Jonson
The Alchemist

Ben Jonson
Volpone

James Joyce
A Portrait of the Artist as a Young Man

John Keats
Selected Poems

Philip Larkin
Selected Poems

D.H. Lawrence
The Rainbow

D.H. Lawrence
Selected Stories

D.H. Lawrence
Sons and Lovers

D.H. Lawrence
Women in Love

Laurie Lee
Cider with Rosie

Christopher Marlowe
Doctor Faustus

Arthur Miller
Death of a Salesman

John Milton
Paradise Lost Bks I & II

John Milton
Paradise Lost IV & IX

Sean O'Casey
Juno and the Paycock

George Orwell
Nineteen Eighty-four

John Osborne
Look Back in Anger

Wilfred Owen
Selected Poems

Harold Pinter
The Caretaker

Sylvia Plath
Selected Works

Alexander Pope
Selected Poems

Jean Rhys
Wide Sargasso Sea

William Shakespeare
As You Like It

William Shakespeare
Coriolanus

William Shakespeare
Henry IV Pt 1

William Shakespeare
Henry IV Pt II

William Shakespeare
Henry V

William Shakespeare
Julius Caesar

William Shakespeare
Measure for Measure

William Shakespeare
Much Ado About Nothing

William Shakespeare
A Midsummer Night's Dream

William Shakespeare
Richard II

William Shakespeare
Richard III

William Shakespeare
Sonnets

William Shakespeare
The Taming of the Shrew

William Shakespeare
The Tempest

William Shakespeare
The Winter's Tale

George Bernard Shaw
Arms and the Man

George Bernard Shaw
Saint Joan

Richard Brinsley Sheridan
The Rivals

R.C. Sherriff
Journey's End

Muriel Spark
The Prime of Miss Jean Brodie

John Steinbeck
The Grapes of Wrath

John Steinbeck
The Pearl

Tom Stoppard
Rosencrantz and Guildenstern are Dead

Jonathan Swift
Gulliver's Travels

John Millington Synge
The Playboy of the Western World

W.M. Thackeray
Vanity Fair

Mark Twain
Huckleberry Finn

Virgil
The Aeneid

Derek Walcott
Selected Poems

Oscar Wilde
The Importance of Being Earnest

Tennessee Williams
Cat on a Hot Tin Roof

Tennessee Williams
The Glass Menagerie

Tennessee Williams
A Streetcar Named Desire

Virginia Woolf
Mrs Dalloway

Virginia Woolf
To the Lighthouse

William Wordsworth
Selected Poems

W.B. Yeats
Selected Poems

York Notes – the Ultimate Literature Guides

York Notes are recognised as the best literature study guides.
If you have enjoyed using this book and have found it useful, you
can now order others directly from us – simply follow the ordering
instructions below.

HOW TO ORDER

Decide which title(s) you require and then order in one of the following
ways:

Booksellers

All titles available from good bookstores.

By post

List the title(s) you require in the space provided overleaf,
select your method of payment, complete your name and
address details and return your completed order form and
payment to:

> *Addison Wesley Longman Ltd*
> *PO BOX 88*
> *Harlow*
> *Essex CM19 5SR*

By phone

Call our Customer Information Centre on 01279 623923 to
place your order, quoting mail number: HEYN1.

By fax

Complete the order form overleaf, ensuring you fill in your
name and address details and method of payment, and fax it
to us on 01279 414130.

By e-mail

E-mail your order to us on awlhe.orders@awl.co.uk listing
title(s) and quantity required and providing full name and
address details as requested overleaf. Please quote mail
number: HEYN1. Please do not send credit card details by
e-mail.

York Notes Order Form

Titles required:

Quantity	Title/ISBN	Price

Sub total _____

Please add £2.50 postage & packing _____

(*P & P is free for orders over £50*) _____

Total _____

Mail no: HEYN1

Your Name _____

Your Address _____

Postcode _____ Telephone _____

Method of payment

☐ I enclose a cheque or a P/O for £_____ made payable to Addison Wesley Longman Ltd

☐ Please charge my Visa/Access/AMEX/Diners Club card

Number _____ Expiry Date _____

Signature _____ Date _____

(please ensure that the address given above is the same as for your credit card)

Prices and other details are correct at time of going to press but may change without notice. All orders are subject to status.

☐ *Please tick this box if you would like a complete listing of Longman Study Guides (suitable for GCSE and A-level students)*

🌹 York Press

📖 Longman

Addison Wesley Longman